Healing Your In *Child*

Cognitive Behavioral Therapy Strategies to Address Trauma and Abandonment Wounds | How to Unlock Emotional Freedom and Self-Love

By

Samantha Stevens

Disclaimer

This book is not intended to provide medical advice. It is based on the author's personal experience and is designed to offer advice and strategies for readers seeking to heal their inner child.

Table of Contents

Chapter 1: Introduction

The concept of inner child healing has gained significant attention in recent years as people have come to realize that the wounds of their childhood can impact their adult lives. These wounds can result from different types of childhood experiences, such as neglect, abuse, or abandonment. The wounds may be physical or emotional, and they can affect a person's self-esteem, relationships, and emotional regulation.

The term "inner child" refers to the emotional and psychological aspect of a person's childhood self that remains within them into adulthood. The inner child may represent the vulnerable, wounded, and neglected aspects of a person's past. It is important to address and heal these inner child wounds to overcome their impact on adult life.

The impact of childhood wounds can be profound and long-lasting. It can affect a person's ability to form healthy relationships, pursue their goals, and experience happiness and fulfillment. Unresolved inner child wounds can lead to negative thought patterns, emotional distress, and a sense of unworthiness.

In this book, we will explore the concept of the inner child and how it is related to childhood wounds. We will also discuss the benefits of cognitive-behavioral therapy (CBT) as a tool for healing inner child wounds. CBT is a form of psychotherapy that focuses on changing negative thought patterns and behaviors to promote positive mental health and well-being. We will also introduce a range of other tools and techniques, such as mindfulness, visualization, and art therapy, that can aid in the healing process.

We will begin by exploring the impact of childhood wounds on adult life. We will identify common types of childhood wounds and how they can manifest in adult life. We will discuss the negative effects of unaddressed childhood wounds on relationships, self-esteem, and emotional regulation.

Next, we will introduce cognitive-behavioral therapy as an effective tool for healing inner child wounds. We will discuss the principles of CBT and how they can be adapted to address inner child wounds. We will provide case studies to illustrate the effectiveness of CBT in healing inner child wounds.

In subsequent chapters, we will introduce a range of tools and techniques for inner child healing. We will explore the benefits of each technique and provide step-by-step instructions for implementation. We will also highlight the importance of self-care in the inner child healing process.

We will discuss common obstacles to inner child healing, such as resistance to change and fear of vulnerability. We will provide strategies for overcoming these obstacles and highlight the importance of perseverance and self-compassion in the healing journey.

Throughout the book, we will focus on the importance of identifying and addressing inner child wounds as a means of unlocking emotional freedom and self-love. We will provide encouragement and guidance for readers on their inner child healing journey, as well as additional resources and recommendations for continued growth and healing.

What is the Inner Child?

The inner child is the emotional and psychological aspect of a person's childhood self that remains within them into adulthood. It can represent the vulnerable, wounded, and neglected aspects of a person's past. The inner child is part of a person that carries their childhood experiences, emotions, and beliefs.

The concept of the inner child is based on the idea that our childhood experiences shape who we are as adults. These experiences can have a profound impact on our sense of self, relationships, and emotional well-being. The inner child can be wounded by a variety of experiences, including neglect, abuse, and abandonment.

Inner child healing is the process of identifying and addressing these wounds to promote emotional healing and growth. It involves recognizing the impact of childhood experiences on adult life and taking steps to heal and integrate the wounded aspects of the inner child. Inner child healing is an essential component of overall emotional well-being and can lead to increased self-esteem, healthier relationships, and greater emotional regulation.

Understanding the importance of inner child healing is critical for promoting emotional growth and healing. By recognizing and addressing the wounds of the inner child, individuals can overcome negative thought patterns, emotional distress, and feelings of unworthiness. Inner child healing can help individuals cultivate greater self-love, emotional resilience, and inner peace. It is a powerful tool for unlocking emotional freedom and creating a fulfilling life.

Childhood Wounds and Their Impact

Childhood wounds can have a profound impact on adult life. They can lead to negative thought patterns, emotional distress, and a sense of unworthiness. Identifying these wounds and their impact is the first step in the inner child healing process.

Impact of childhood trauma and abandonment wounds on adult life

Childhood trauma and abandonment wounds can have significant long-term effects on a person's emotional and psychological well-being. Trauma can result from a variety of experiences, such as physical or sexual abuse, neglect, or witnessing violence. Abandonment wounds can result from experiences such as parental divorce, neglect, or emotional abandonment.

The impact of childhood trauma and abandonment wounds can manifest in a variety of ways, including:

- Negative thought patterns: Childhood wounds can lead to negative beliefs about oneself and the world. These negative beliefs can become ingrained in a person's thought patterns and affect their self-esteem and emotional well-being.

- Emotional distress: Childhood wounds can result in emotional distress, such as anxiety, depression, or anger. These emotions can be triggered by events or experiences that remind a person of their childhood wounds.

- Relationship difficulties: Childhood wounds can impact a person's ability to form healthy relationships. They may struggle with trust, emotional intimacy, or communication, leading to relationship difficulties.

- Self-esteem issues: Childhood wounds can lead to a sense of unworthiness or a lack of self-esteem. This can affect a person's confidence, self-worth, and ability to pursue their goals.

Identifying common types of childhood wounds

Identifying the types of childhood wounds is essential for understanding their impact on adult life. The following are some of the most common types of childhood wounds:

- Neglect: Neglect can result from a lack of attention or care from caregivers. It can lead to feelings of abandonment, worthlessness, and a lack of trust.

- Abuse: Abuse can take many forms, including physical, sexual, and emotional abuse. It can lead to trauma, fear, and negative self-beliefs.

- Abandonment: Abandonment can result from experiences such as parental divorce, emotional abandonment, or being placed in foster care. It can lead to feelings of rejection, shame, and a lack of trust.

- Enmeshment: Enmeshment occurs when a child is overly involved in their parents' emotional lives. It can lead to difficulties in forming healthy relationships and a lack of emotional boundaries.

- Overprotection: Overprotection can lead to a lack of confidence, independence, and self-esteem. It can also lead to difficulties in forming healthy relationships and pursuing goals.

Cognitive Behavioral Therapy for Inner Child Healing

Cognitive-behavioral therapy (CBT) is a form of psychotherapy that focuses on changing negative thought patterns and behaviors to promote positive mental health and well-being. It can be an effective tool for healing inner child wounds.

Introducing cognitive-behavioral therapy (CBT) as a tool for healing inner child wounds

CBT is a widely used form of therapy that has been shown to be effective in treating a range of mental health conditions, including depression, anxiety, and trauma. It is a goal-oriented therapy that focuses on the present and future rather than the past. CBT aims to identify negative thought patterns and behaviors and replace them with positive ones.

CBT can be adapted to address inner child wounds by focusing on the negative beliefs and thought patterns that result from childhood wounds. By identifying these negative beliefs and patterns, individuals can challenge and replace them with positive, healthy ones. This process can lead to increased self-esteem, emotional regulation, and overall well-being.

Benefits of CBT for inner child healing

CBT offers several benefits for inner child healing, including:

- Empowerment: CBT empowers individuals to take control of their thoughts and emotions. It teaches individuals skills and techniques for challenging negative beliefs and replacing them with positive ones.

- Goal-orientation: CBT is a goal-oriented therapy that focuses on the present and future. It helps individuals set achievable goals for their healing journey and provides them with the tools to achieve those goals.

- Flexibility: CBT can be adapted to address a wide range of inner child wounds. It can be tailored to the individual's specific needs and can be used in conjunction with other therapies and techniques.

- Evidence-based: CBT is a well-researched and evidence-based form of therapy. Numerous studies have shown its effectiveness in treating a range of mental health conditions, including trauma.

CBT can be an effective tool for healing inner child wounds by identifying and challenging negative beliefs and thought patterns. By replacing these negative patterns with positive ones, individuals can overcome the impact of childhood wounds and unlock emotional freedom and self-love.

Chapter 2: Understanding Inner Child Wounds

In this chapter, we will explore the different types of childhood wounds and their impact on adult life. We will also examine how childhood wounds can manifest in adult behaviors, thought patterns, and emotions.

Types of Childhood Wounds

Childhood wounds are experiences that can have a significant impact on a person's emotional and psychological well-being. These experiences can range from neglect and abandonment to physical, sexual, and emotional abuse. In this section, we will explore the different types of childhood wounds and their impact on adult life.

Neglect

Neglect occurs when a caregiver fails to provide adequate care or attention to a child's physical, emotional, or psychological needs. Neglect can take many forms, such as:

1. Physical neglect: Failing to provide adequate food, clothing, or shelter

2. Emotional neglect: Failing to provide emotional support, affection, or attention
3. Medical neglect: Failing to provide necessary medical care or attention

Neglect can have a profound impact on a child's emotional and psychological well-being. Children who experience neglect may feel abandoned, worthless, and unimportant. They may struggle with self-esteem and have difficulty forming healthy relationships. Neglect can also lead to emotional distress and may impact a child's ability to regulate their emotions.

Abuse

Abuse can take many forms, including physical, sexual, and emotional abuse. Physical abuse involves the use of physical force that results in injury or harm. Sexual abuse involves any sexual activity between an adult and a child. Emotional abuse involves the use of words, gestures, or actions that harm a child's emotional well-being. Abuse can have a significant impact on a child's emotional and psychological well-being. Some of the effects of abuse include:

1. Physical effects: Injuries, bruises, or other physical trauma
2. Emotional effects: Anxiety, depression, or other emotional distress
3. Behavioral effects: Aggression, withdrawal, or other behavioral changes

Abuse can lead to trauma, fear, and negative self-beliefs. Children who experience abuse may struggle with trust, emotional intimacy, and forming healthy relationships.

Abandonment

Abandonment can result from experiences such as parental divorce, emotional abandonment, or being placed in foster care. Abandonment can have a significant impact on a child's emotional and psychological well-being. Some of the effects of abandonment include:

1. Emotional distress: Anxiety, depression, or other emotional distress
2. Relationship difficulties: Difficulty forming healthy relationships or struggling with trust
3. Self-esteem issues: A sense of unworthiness or a lack of self-esteem

Children who experience abandonment may struggle with feelings of rejection, shame, and fear of abandonment. They may also have difficulty regulating their emotions and may struggle with feelings of sadness or loneliness.

Other Types of Childhood Wounds

Other types of childhood wounds can include:

1. Enmeshment: Occurs when a child is overly involved in their parents' emotional lives. It can lead to difficulties forming healthy relationships and a lack of emotional boundaries.
2. Overprotection: This can lead to a lack of confidence, independence, and self-esteem. It can also lead to difficulties forming healthy relationships and pursuing goals.

By recognizing the different types of childhood wounds, individuals can begin to understand how their past experiences may be impacting their current emotional and psychological well-being. This awareness is the first step in the inner child healing process. It can also help individuals identify patterns in their behaviors, thoughts, and emotions that may be related to childhood wounds.

Impact of Childhood Wounds

Childhood wounds, also known as adverse childhood experiences (ACEs), are traumatic events that occur during the early years of a person's life. These experiences may include emotional, physical, or sexual abuse, neglect, loss of a parent, domestic violence, or other adverse events. The long-lasting effects of these experiences can be far-reaching, extending into adulthood and impacting various aspects of life.

Effects on Self-Esteem

Internalized Negative Beliefs

Childhood wounds often lead to the development of internalized negative beliefs about oneself. As children, we are vulnerable and dependent on our caregivers for love, support, and validation. When caregivers fail to provide these essential needs, children may internalize the message that they are unworthy, unlovable, or inadequate. This negative self-image persists into adulthood, resulting in low self-esteem and a diminished sense of self-worth.

Difficulty with Self-compassion

Individuals who have experienced childhood wounds often struggle with self-compassion, which can further damage their self-esteem. They may find it difficult to be kind and gentle with themselves, often resorting to self-criticism and blame when confronted with setbacks or failure. This lack of self-compassion exacerbates feelings of inadequacy, making it challenging to develop healthy self-esteem.

Perfectionism

Another consequence of childhood wounds is the development of perfectionism. In an attempt to gain approval or validation from caregivers, children may adopt an unhealthy drive to be perfect. Perfectionism can lead to a relentless pursuit of high standards, which, when not met, results in feelings of failure and low self-esteem. The fear of making mistakes and the need to be perfect can hinder personal growth and self-acceptance.

Effects on Relationships

Attachment Issues

Childhood wounds can lead to insecure attachment styles, which can greatly impact an individual's ability to form and maintain healthy relationships. Insecure attachment styles include anxious, avoidant, and disorganized attachment, which are characterized by fear of abandonment, emotional distance, and chaotic relational patterns, respectively. These attachment issues can make it difficult for individuals to trust, connect, and feel secure in their relationships.

Codependency

Another effect of childhood wounds on relationships is the development of codependency, a pattern of behavior in which an individual relies on others for their emotional needs and sense of self-worth. Codependency can result in unhealthy, one-sided relationships, where one person prioritizes the needs of others over their own, often leading to resentment and dissatisfaction.

Repetition of Unhealthy Patterns

Individuals who have experienced childhood wounds may unconsciously repeat unhealthy patterns in their adult relationships. This repetition may manifest as choosing partners who are emotionally unavailable or abusive, re-enacting childhood traumas, or engaging in self-sabotaging behaviors. This cycle of unhealthy relationships can reinforce negative beliefs about oneself and perpetuate the effects of childhood wounds.

Effects on Emotional Regulation

Emotional Dysregulation

Childhood wounds can significantly impact an individual's ability to regulate their emotions effectively. Emotional dysregulation is characterized by intense, rapid shifts in mood, difficulty soothing oneself, and impulsive behavior. Individuals who have experienced childhood trauma may struggle to recognize, understand, and manage their emotions, leading to emotional outbursts, withdrawal, or self-destructive behaviors.

Increased Vulnerability to Mental Health Issues

The effects of childhood wounds on emotional regulation can increase vulnerability to mental health issues such as anxiety, depression, and post-traumatic stress disorder (PTSD). These disorders can further exacerbate emotional dysregulation and create a cycle of emotional instability. The inability to manage emotions effectively may result in an increased likelihood of engaging in maladaptive coping strategies, such as substance abuse or self-harm, to numb emotional pain.

Difficulty with Emotional Intimacy

The impact of childhood wounds on emotional regulation can also lead to challenges with emotional intimacy in relationships. Individuals who have experienced childhood trauma may struggle to express their emotions, as they may have learned to suppress their feelings as a coping mechanism during their early years. This inability to openly share emotions can hinder the development of deep, meaningful connections with others and contribute to feelings of isolation and loneliness.

Examples of How Childhood Wounds Manifest

Childhood wounds, or adverse childhood experiences, can have lasting impacts on an individual's life. These traumatic events often shape a person's behaviors, thought patterns, and emotions, creating a complex web of interconnected issues that persist into adulthood. This paper will explore in detail how childhood wounds can manifest through various behaviors, thought patterns, and emotions, providing examples to illustrate the potential consequences of these early traumatic experiences.

Behaviors

Self-sabotaging Behaviors

One way childhood wounds can manifest is through self-sabotaging behaviors. These behaviors may include procrastination, engaging in unhealthy relationships, or sabotaging opportunities for success. For example, an individual with a history of childhood abuse may unconsciously avoid applying for promotions at work, fearing that they are unworthy of success or that they will be exposed as fraud. This self-sabotaging behavior may be a means of protecting oneself from perceived failure or rejection.

Substance Abuse

Another common behavioral manifestation of childhood wounds is substance abuse. Individuals who have experienced trauma in their early years may turn to drugs or alcohol as a means of coping with their emotional pain or escaping from difficult memories. Substance abuse can provide temporary relief from distressing emotions but often leads to addiction and further complications in an individual's life.

Disordered Eating

Childhood wounds can also lead to disordered eating behaviors. These may include restrictive dieting, binge eating, purging, or excessive exercise, and they can be rooted in a desire to exert control or gain a sense of self-worth. For example, an individual who experienced neglect in their early years may develop an eating disorder as a means of asserting control over their body and environment or as a way to cope with feelings of emptiness or inadequacy.

Thought Patterns

Catastrophizing

Catastrophizing is a thought pattern that involves exaggerating the potential negative outcomes of a situation or assuming the worst will happen. This cognitive distortion can be a result of childhood wounds, as individuals who have experienced early trauma may develop a heightened sense of fear or vulnerability. For example, a child who grew up witnessing domestic violence may become an adult who catastrophizes every argument in their relationship, fearing that it will escalate to physical aggression.

Negative Self-talk

Negative self-talk, or the internal dialogue that is critical and self-deprecating, is another thought pattern that can stem from childhood wounds. Individuals who have experienced trauma may internalize the negative messages they received from caregivers or others, leading to a constant stream of self-criticism and doubt. For example, a person who was repeatedly belittled or criticized by their parents may grow up with a persistent belief that they are incompetent, unlovable, or unworthy.

Black-and-white Thinking

Black-and-white thinking, also known as all-or-nothing thinking, is a thought pattern characterized by viewing situations, people, or oneself in absolutes without acknowledging the complexity or nuance that exists in reality. This cognitive distortion can be rooted in childhood wounds, as individuals who experienced trauma may have developed a need for certainty and control in response to the chaos or unpredictability of their early environment. For example, an individual who experienced sexual abuse may view all romantic partners as either entirely good or entirely bad without recognizing the possibility of a mix of positive and negative qualities.

Emotions

Chronic Anxiety

Chronic anxiety is a common emotional manifestation of childhood wounds. Individuals who have experienced trauma in their early years may develop a heightened sense of fear or worry as their nervous system becomes sensitized to potential threats. This chronic anxiety can manifest as persistent feelings of unease, restlessness, or apprehension and can impact various aspects of an individual's life, including their relationships, work, and overall well-being. For example, a person who experienced emotional neglect as a child may develop chronic anxiety around abandonment or rejection, leading to constant worry about their relationships and a fear of being alone.

Emotional Numbness

Emotional numbness, or the inability to feel or express emotions, can also be a manifestation of childhood wounds. This emotional detachment can be a defense mechanism that develops in response to overwhelming or chronic trauma as a means of self-protection. For example, a child who experienced physical abuse may learn to numb their emotions to avoid feeling pain, fear, or sadness. This emotional numbness can persist into adulthood, making it difficult to connect with others and experience joy or fulfillment.

Intense and Unstable Emotions

In contrast to emotional numbness, some individuals with childhood wounds may experience intense and unstable emotions. This emotional dysregulation can be a consequence of early trauma, as the individual may not have had the opportunity to learn healthy emotional regulation skills from their caregivers. For example, a child who grew up in a chaotic home environment with frequent emotional outbursts from their parents may develop a pattern of intense, rapidly shifting emotions that are difficult to manage and control.

Childhood wounds can have far-reaching and long-lasting impacts on an individual's behaviors, thought patterns, and emotions. These manifestations of early trauma can create a cycle of self-defeating beliefs and behaviors, perpetuating the pain and suffering caused by the initial adverse experiences. However, it is crucial to recognize that healing and growth are possible. Through therapeutic intervention, self-awareness, and support from loved ones, individuals can work to break free from the grip of their childhood wounds and develop healthier patterns of thinking, feeling, and behaving. By addressing the root causes of these issues and fostering resilience and self-compassion, individuals who have experienced childhood wounds can begin to reclaim their lives and build a brighter future.

Chapter 3: Cognitive-Behavioral Therapy Strategies for Inner Child Healing

Inner child healing has become a focal point in the realm of personal development and therapy, as it addresses the root causes of many emotional, behavioral, and cognitive issues that persist into adulthood. Cognitive-Behavioral Therapy (CBT), a widely-used therapeutic approach, offers various strategies that can be tailored to support inner child healing. In this chapter, we will explore the principles of CBT, how they can be adapted for inner child work, and provide case studies to demonstrate the potential benefits of using CBT for inner child healing. By understanding and implementing these strategies, individuals can embark on a transformative journey of self-discovery, healing, and personal growth.

CBT Principles

Cognitive-Behavioral Therapy (CBT) is a well-established and evidence-based therapeutic approach that focuses on the interplay between an individual's thoughts, emotions, and behaviors. The primary goal of CBT is to help individuals identify and modify maladaptive thought patterns and behaviors, ultimately leading to improved emotional well-being and overall functioning. CBT is founded upon several key principles that guide its methodology and inform its techniques.

1. The Cognitive Model: At the core of CBT is the cognitive model, which posits that an individual's thoughts, rather than external events, are the primary determinants of their

emotions and behaviors. According to this model, it is not the situation itself that causes emotional distress but rather the individual's interpretation of the situation. By changing one's thought patterns and beliefs, an individual can ultimately change how they feel and behave in response to various situations.

2. Structure and Goal Orientation: CBT is a structured, goal-oriented therapy that emphasizes the importance of setting specific, measurable, and achievable objectives for treatment. This approach allows both the therapist and the you to track progress and continuously evaluate the effectiveness of the therapeutic interventions. CBT typically involves a collaborative relationship between the therapist and the you, with both parties actively working together to identify problems, set goals, and develop strategies for change.

3. Time-Limited and Present-Focused: CBT is generally a time-limited therapy, with most treatment plans ranging from 8 to 20 sessions. The therapy focuses on addressing current issues and problems rather than extensively exploring the individual's past. While past experiences may be considered in the context of understanding the development of maladaptive thought patterns and behaviors, the primary focus remains on helping the individual develop skills and strategies to cope effectively with their present-day challenges.

4. Skill Development and Self-Efficacy: CBT emphasizes the importance of skill development and self-efficacy in achieving lasting change. Through various techniques and exercises, individuals learn to identify and challenge their negative thought patterns, develop more adaptive ways of thinking, and engage in behavioral activation to improve their overall well-being. As you develop these skills and experience success in implementing them, they begin to build confidence in their ability to effectively manage their emotions and cope with life's challenges, ultimately promoting long-term growth and change.

Identifying Negative Thought Patterns

One of the foundational aspects of CBT is the identification of negative thought patterns, also known as cognitive distortions. These distorted thoughts often contribute to emotional distress and maladaptive behaviors, making it essential for individuals to recognize and address them in order to facilitate lasting change. The following sections will explore the process of identifying negative thought patterns and the various types of cognitive distortions that individuals may encounter.

Types of Cognitive Distortions

There are several types of cognitive distortions that individuals may experience, including:

- All-or-nothing thinking: Viewing situations, people, or oneself in extreme, black-and-white terms, without acknowledging the complexity and nuance that exists in reality.

- Catastrophizing: Exaggerating the potential negative outcomes of a situation or assuming the worst will happen.

- Emotional reasoning: Believing that one's emotions are an accurate reflection of reality, even when there is evidence to the contrary (e.g., "I feel like a failure, so I must be a failure").

- Overgeneralization: Drawing broad, negative conclusions based on a single event or piece of evidence.

- Personalization: Attributing external events or other people's behaviors to oneself, assuming personal responsibility for things that are beyond one's control.

Thought Monitoring

Thought monitoring is a key technique in CBT that involves observing and recording one's thoughts, particularly those that arise during emotionally challenging situations.

By keeping a thought record or journal, individuals can begin to identify recurring negative thought patterns and recognize the triggers that lead to these patterns. Thought monitoring can help individuals gain insight into their cognitive distortions and develop a deeper understanding of their thought processes.

Identifying Core Beliefs

In addition to recognizing cognitive distortions, CBT also focuses on identifying and challenging core beliefs. Core beliefs are deeply held assumptions about oneself, others, and the world that often develop during childhood and shape an individual's thoughts, emotions, and behaviors. These beliefs may be negative or limiting, such as "I am unworthy" or "People cannot be trusted." By identifying and examining these core beliefs, individuals can begin to understand how these beliefs contribute to their negative thought patterns and work on challenging and changing them.

Replacing Negative Thoughts with Positive Ones

Once negative thought patterns have been identified, the next step in CBT is to replace these thoughts with more positive and balanced ones. This process is essential for promoting emotional well-being and facilitating lasting change.

Cognitive Restructuring

Cognitive restructuring is a fundamental technique in CBT that involves challenging and reframing negative thought patterns. This process includes identifying cognitive distortions, evaluating the evidence that supports or contradicts these thoughts, and generating alternative, more balanced thoughts. Cognitive restructuring helps individuals develop more adaptive thought patterns, which can lead to improved emotional well-being and more effective coping strategies.

Socratic Questioning

Socratic questioning is another technique used in CBT to help individuals challenge and replace their negative thoughts. This method involves asking a series of open-ended questions designed to encourage the individual to critically examine their beliefs and assumptions. Through Socratic questioning, individuals can uncover the inconsistencies and errors in their thinking, ultimately leading to the development of more balanced and rational thought patterns.

Positive Affirmations and Visualization

In addition to cognitive restructuring and Socratic questioning, individuals can also use positive affirmations and visualization techniques to help replace negative thoughts with positive ones. Positive affirmations involve repeating positive statements to oneself, while visualization involves imagining oneself in a positive and successful situation. Both techniques can help to counteract the effects of negative thinking and foster a more optimistic mindset.

Behavioral Activation

Behavioral activation is a key component of CBT that focuses on helping individuals engage in activities that promote positive emotions and improve overall well-being. This approach is based on the premise that engaging in rewarding and meaningful activities can counteract the negative effects of cognitive distortions and emotional distress, ultimately leading to lasting change.

Identifying Values and Goals

The first step in behavioral activation is identifying one's values and goals, which can provide a sense of direction and purpose for the individual. By clarifying what is truly important and meaningful to them, individuals can begin to develop a roadmap for engaging in activities that align with their values and support their well-being.

Activity Scheduling

Activity scheduling is a technique used in behavioral activation that involves planning and scheduling specific activities that align with one's values and goals. By setting aside time for these activities, individuals can ensure that they prioritize their well-being and take steps toward achieving their desired outcomes.

Gradual Exposure

For individuals who experience anxiety or fear related to certain activities or situations, gradual exposure can be an effective component of behavioral activation. This technique involves gradually and systematically facing feared situations, starting with the least anxiety-provoking situations and progressively moving toward more challenging ones. Through gradual exposure, individuals can build confidence in their ability to cope with anxiety and develop a greater sense of mastery over their fears.

Problem-Solving and Coping Skills Training

Behavioral activation may also involve teaching individuals problem-solving and coping skills to help them effectively navigate challenges and setbacks. These skills can include stress management techniques, communication strategies, and assertiveness training, among others. By developing and refining these skills, individuals can become more resilient and better equipped to cope with the obstacles they encounter in their pursuit of well-being and personal growth.

Monitoring Progress and Adjusting Strategies

An essential aspect of behavioral activation is regularly monitoring one's progress and adjusting strategies as needed. This may involve evaluating the effectiveness of specific activities in promoting positive emotions, identifying barriers to engagement, and troubleshooting any difficulties that arise. By continuously assessing and refining their approach, individuals can optimize their behavioral activation efforts and maximize the benefits they derive from engaging in value-aligned activities.

Adapting CBT for Inner Child Work

Addressing Negative Self-Talk

Negative self-talk is a common manifestation of unresolved childhood wounds and can significantly contribute to feelings of low self-esteem, self-doubt, and self-criticism. In the context of inner child work, addressing negative self-talk involves recognizing and challenging the self-defeating thoughts and beliefs that stem from one's early experiences. CBT offers several techniques for addressing negative self-talk, including:

a. Identifying the Source of Negative Self-Talk: To effectively address negative self-talk, it is essential to identify the source of these thoughts and beliefs. This may involve exploring one's childhood experiences and examining the messages and expectations that were internalized during this time. Identifying the source of negative self-talk can provide valuable insights into the root causes of one's self-defeating thoughts and beliefs, ultimately enabling more targeted and effective interventions.

b. Cognitive Restructuring: Cognitive restructuring is a CBT technique that can be effectively adapted for inner child work to help individuals challenge and reframe their negative self-talk. This process involves identifying the cognitive distortions that underlie one's self-defeating thoughts, evaluating the evidence for and against these thoughts, and generating alternative, more balanced thoughts. By actively challenging and reframing one's negative self-talk, individuals can begin to develop a more positive and compassionate relationship with their inner child.

c. Developing Self-Compassion: An essential aspect of addressing negative self-talk in inner child work is developing self-compassion. Self-compassion involves cultivating a kind, understanding, and non-judgmental attitude toward oneself, particularly during times of suffering or failure. By practicing self-compassion, individuals can counteract the effects of negative self-talk and create a safe and supportive internal environment for their inner child to heal and grow.

Coping With Emotions

Unresolved childhood wounds can often manifest as intense and overwhelming emotions in adulthood. As such, learning to cope effectively with emotions is a crucial aspect of inner child work. CBT offers several strategies for managing emotions, including:

a. Emotional Awareness and Labeling: Emotional awareness involves recognizing and acknowledging one's emotions without judgment. This is a critical skill for inner child work, as it enables individuals to identify the emotions that arise in response to their unresolved childhood issues. By developing emotional awareness and accurately labeling their emotions, individuals can better understand the impact of their childhood experiences on their emotional landscape.

b. Cognitive Distancing: Cognitive distancing is a CBT technique that can help individuals cope with intense emotions by creating mental space between themselves and their emotional experiences. This technique involves viewing one's emotions from an objective, observer perspective rather than becoming consumed by the emotions themselves. Cognitive distancing can help individuals gain perspective on their emotions and develop a greater sense of emotional control.

c. Emotional Regulation Techniques: CBT offers several emotional regulation techniques that can be adapted for inner child work, including deep breathing exercises, progressive muscle relaxation, and mindfulness meditation. These techniques can help individuals manage their emotional responses to unresolved childhood issues, enabling them to process and work through their emotions in a healthy and constructive manner.

d. Expressive Writing: Expressive writing is a therapeutic technique that involves writing about one's thoughts and feelings related to a specific event or experience. In the context of inner child work, expressive writing can help individuals process and make sense of their unresolved childhood emotions, ultimately promoting healing and emotional well-being.

Changing Relationship Patterns

Unresolved childhood wounds can significantly impact an individual's relationship patterns, often leading to dysfunctional dynamics and unhealthy attachments. CBT can be adapted for inner child work to help individuals recognize and change their maladaptive relationship patterns, including:

a. Identifying Relationship Patterns: The first step in changing relationship patterns is to identify the specific dynamics and behaviors that contribute to unhealthy relationships. This may involve exploring one's past relationships and examining the themes and patterns that emerge. By identifying the underlying causes and triggers of their relationship patterns, individuals can develop a better understanding of how their unresolved childhood issues influence their interpersonal dynamics.

b. Attachment Theory and Inner Child Work: Attachment theory posits that early childhood experiences, particularly those involving one's primary caregivers, play a significant role in shaping an individual's attachment style and subsequent relationship patterns. By examining one's attachment style and exploring the childhood experiences that contributed to its development, individuals can gain valuable insights into the root causes of their relationship patterns and work to address these issues through inner child work.

c. Communication Skills Training: Effective communication is a critical component of healthy relationships, and developing these skills can be a valuable aspect of inner child work. CBT offers several communication skills training techniques, such as active listening, assertiveness training, and conflict resolution strategies, that can be adapted for inner child work to help individuals improve their interpersonal dynamics and foster healthier relationships.

d. Setting Boundaries: Setting healthy boundaries is another important aspect of changing relationship patterns in inner child work. Boundaries involve establishing clear limits and expectations in relationships, allowing individuals to protect themselves emotionally and maintain a sense of autonomy and control. By learning to set and enforce boundaries, individuals can create a safe and supportive environment for their inner child to heal and grow.

Case Studies

Case Study 1: Overcoming Childhood Trauma and Anxiety

Anna, a 35-year-old woman, sought therapy to address her chronic anxiety and panic attacks, which she believed were rooted in her traumatic childhood experiences. As a child, Anna endured physical and emotional abuse from her parents, leading to feelings of insecurity and constant fear. Her therapist utilized CBT techniques to help Anna process her childhood trauma and alleviate her anxiety symptoms.

Initially, the therapist worked with Anna to identify the negative thought patterns and cognitive distortions that were fueling her anxiety. They discovered that Anna's inner child held core beliefs such as "I am not safe" and "I am unlovable." Using cognitive restructuring, Anna learned to challenge and reframe these beliefs with more balanced and compassionate thoughts.

The therapist also guided Anna through exposure therapy to gradually confront and overcome her anxiety-provoking situations. By facing her fears in a controlled and supportive environment, Anna was able to reduce her anxiety and develop a greater sense of mastery and control over her emotions.

As Anna's anxiety decreased, she began to work on developing self-compassion and nurturing her inner child. The therapist used guided imagery and visualization exercises to help Anna create a safe and comforting mental space where she could connect with and care for her inner child.

Throughout the course of her therapy, Anna experienced significant improvements in her anxiety symptoms and developed a deeper understanding of the impact her childhood trauma had on her emotional well-being.

Case Study 2: Addressing Low Self-Esteem and Negative Self-Talk

James, a 28-year-old man, sought therapy to help him overcome his persistent feelings of low self-esteem and negative self-talk. Growing up, James had been repeatedly criticized and belittled by his parents, leading him to internalize feelings of inadequacy and self-doubt. His therapist used CBT techniques to help James address his negative self-talk and build his self-esteem.

The therapist began by helping James identify the sources of his negative self-talk, which were rooted in his childhood experiences. They then worked together to identify the cognitive distortions that were contributing to his low self-esteem, such as all-or-nothing thinking, overgeneralization, and personalization.

Using cognitive restructuring, James learned to challenge and replace his negative self-talk with more balanced and accurate thoughts. The therapist also encouraged James to practice self-compassion and self-acceptance, fostering a more nurturing and supportive internal environment for his inner child.

As James began to develop a more positive self-concept, the therapist introduced behavioral activation techniques to help him engage in activities that aligned with his values and promoted feelings of self-worth. Over time, James noticed a significant improvement in his self-esteem and overall emotional well-being.

Case Study 3: Healing from Childhood Emotional Neglect and Improving Relationships

Sophia, a 42-year-old woman, entered therapy to address her difficulties in maintaining healthy relationships. She had a history of engaging in emotionally unavailable or abusive relationships, which she believed were connected to her experience of emotional neglect during childhood. Her therapist utilized CBT techniques to help Sophia heal her inner child and develop healthier relationship patterns.

The therapist worked with Sophia to explore her attachment style, which was rooted in her childhood experiences of emotional neglect. They discovered that Sophia's inner child held core beliefs such as "I don't deserve love" and "I must be perfect to be loved." By identifying and addressing these beliefs, Sophia was able to gain a better understanding of how her childhood experiences influenced her relationship patterns.

Sophia's therapist then introduced cognitive restructuring techniques to help her challenge and reframe her negative beliefs about herself and her relationships. As Sophia developed a more balanced and positive view of herself, she began to notice improvements in her self-esteem and emotional well-being.

The therapist also taught Sophia communication skills, such as active listening, assertiveness, and conflict resolution strategies, to help her foster healthier and more satisfying relationships. By learning and practicing these skills, Sophia was better equipped to navigate the complexities of interpersonal dynamics and establish more secure and nurturing connections with others.

Additionally, the therapist guided Sophia through setting healthy boundaries in her relationships. This involved establishing clear expectations and limits to protect her emotional well-being and maintain a sense of autonomy and control. By setting and enforcing boundaries, Sophia created a safer environment for her inner child to heal and grow.

Over the course of her therapy, Sophia experienced significant improvements in her relationship patterns and emotional well-being, ultimately fostering a healthier and more fulfilling life.

Conclusion

The case studies presented above demonstrate the versatility and effectiveness of Cognitive-Behavioral Therapy in addressing unresolved childhood wounds and promoting inner child healing. By utilizing CBT techniques such as cognitive restructuring, behavioral activation, communication skills training, and boundary-setting, therapists can help individuals overcome the effects of childhood trauma, improve their self-esteem, and develop healthier relationship patterns.

These case studies illustrate the power of CBT in providing individuals with the tools and insights needed to heal their inner child and create lasting change in their lives. By addressing negative self-talk, coping with emotions, and changing relationship patterns, individuals can foster a safe and supportive internal environment for their inner child to heal, ultimately promoting emotional resilience and overall well-being.

Chapter 4: Tools and Techniques for Inner Child Healing

The journey of inner child healing is a deeply personal and transformative process that requires a compassionate, nurturing, and holistic approach. Throughout this journey, individuals must confront and work through unresolved childhood wounds, develop a healthier relationship with their inner child, and cultivate emotional resilience and well-being. In order to achieve these goals, it is crucial to have a diverse array of tools and techniques that can be tailored to meet each individual's unique needs and challenges.

In this chapter, we will explore a variety of tools and techniques that have been proven effective in supporting the inner child healing process. These methods include mindfulness, visualization, journaling, progressive muscle relaxation, creative expression, self-compassion exercises, and self-care practices. Each of these techniques offers distinct benefits and can be used in combination to address the multifaceted aspects of inner child healing.

Mindfulness practices can help individuals cultivate greater awareness of their thoughts, emotions, and bodily sensations, providing valuable insights into the impact of their childhood experiences on their present emotional landscape. Visualization techniques can be used to create a safe and comforting mental space for the inner child, promoting healing and emotional growth. Journaling exercises offer a powerful means of processing and making sense of one's unresolved childhood emotions and experiences.

In addition to these core techniques, we will also discuss the benefits of progressive muscle relaxation, creative expression, and self-compassion exercises in supporting inner child healing. Furthermore, we will emphasize the importance of self-care in the healing process, as creating a nurturing and supportive environment for the inner child is essential for fostering emotional resilience and well-being.

By exploring and implementing these diverse tools and techniques, individuals can more effectively navigate the complex and often challenging terrain of inner child healing, ultimately promoting lasting growth, self-understanding, and emotional health.

Mindfulness

Mindfulness, a mental state achieved by focusing one's awareness on the present moment, has been widely recognized for its numerous psychological benefits. In the context of inner child healing, mindfulness can play a pivotal role in helping individuals connect with their inner child, unresolved process emotions, and cultivate emotional resilience. In this section, we will explore the benefits of mindfulness for inner child healing and discuss various techniques for practicing mindfulness.

Benefits of Mindfulness for Inner Child Healing

Enhancing Self-Awareness

One of the primary benefits of mindfulness is its ability to promote self-awareness. By practicing mindfulness, individuals can develop a deeper understanding of their thoughts, emotions, and bodily sensations, allowing them to identify and address the impact of their childhood experiences on their present emotional state. This heightened self-awareness can be invaluable in the inner child healing process, as it enables individuals to recognize and work through unresolved childhood wounds.

Emotional Regulation

Mindfulness has been shown to enhance emotional regulation by teaching individuals to observe and accept their emotions without judgment or resistance. By developing the ability to mindfully experience their emotions, individuals can prevent emotional suppression and facilitate the processing of unresolved childhood emotions. This improved emotional regulation is crucial for inner child healing, as it helps individuals create a more nurturing and supportive internal environment for their inner child.

Reducing Stress and Anxiety

The practice of mindfulness has been proven effective in reducing stress and anxiety. Through the cultivation of present-moment awareness, individuals can learn to let go of negative thought patterns and cognitive distortions that often contribute to stress and anxiety. As a result, they can create a more relaxed and peaceful emotional state, which is essential for fostering a safe space for their inner child to heal and grow.

Cultivating Self-Compassion

Mindfulness encourages the development of self-compassion by teaching individuals to approach their thoughts and emotions with kindness and understanding. By practicing self-compassion, individuals can learn to forgive themselves for past mistakes and provide the loving support their inner child needs to heal from childhood wounds. This compassionate approach to inner child healing can promote lasting emotional well-being and resilience.

Techniques for Practicing Mindfulness

Mindful Breathing

Mindful breathing is a fundamental mindfulness technique that involves focusing one's attention on the breath. To practice mindful breathing, find a comfortable and quiet place to sit or lie down. Close your eyes and take a few deep breaths, noticing the sensation of the air entering and leaving your body. As you continue to breathe, allow your breath to return to its natural rhythm and simply observe it without trying to control or alter it. If your mind begins to wander, gently bring your focus back to your breath. Practicing mindful breathing regularly can help individuals develop greater present-moment awareness and emotional regulation, supporting their inner child healing journey.

Body Scan Meditation

Body scan meditation is another mindfulness technique that can be particularly helpful for individuals working on inner child healing. This practice involves systematically bringing one's attention to different parts of the body and observing any sensations or emotions that may arise. To practice a body scan meditation, find a comfortable position and close your eyes. Beginning at the top of your head, slowly scan your body, moving your attention downward through your face, neck, shoulders, arms, chest, abdomen, hips, legs, and feet. As you scan each body part, observe any sensations or emotions you may experience without judgment or resistance. This practice can help individuals develop greater self-awareness and emotional regulation, enhancing their ability to process unresolved childhood emotions.

Mindful Walking

Mindful walking is a mindfulness technique that can be easily integrated into one's daily routine. To practice mindful walking, choose a location where you can walk comfortably and without distraction. Begin walking at a slow and relaxed pace, focusing your attention on the sensations in your feet as they make contact with the ground. You may also choose to synchronize your breath with your steps, inhaling as you step with one foot and exhaling as you step with the other. As you walk, maintain your awareness of the present moment and gently bring your focus back to your steps if your mind begins to wander. Mindful walking can serve as a powerful tool for cultivating present-moment awareness and reducing stress, creating a more supportive environment for inner child healing.

Loving-Kindness Meditation

Loving-kindness meditation, also known as metta meditation, is a mindfulness practice that focuses on cultivating feelings of love and compassion for oneself and others. This practice can be particularly beneficial for individuals working on inner child healing, as it helps to develop self-compassion and nurture their inner child. To practice loving-kindness meditation, find a comfortable position and close your eyes. Begin by focusing your attention on your heart center and silently reciting phrases such as "May I be happy, may I be healthy, may I be safe, and may I be at ease." After a few minutes, expand your focus to include others, such as loved ones, acquaintances, and even those with whom you may have conflict. Continue to silently recite the phrases, wishing happiness and well-being for all beings. This practice can help individuals develop a more compassionate and supportive relationship with their inner child, promoting emotional healing and resilience.

Mindfulness-Based Stress Reduction (MBSR)

Mindfulness-Based Stress Reduction (MBSR) is an evidence-based, structured mindfulness program developed by Dr. Jon Kabat-Zinn at the University of Massachusetts Medical Center. MBSR incorporates mindfulness techniques such as mindful breathing, body scan meditation, and mindful movement to help individuals reduce stress, improve emotional regulation, and cultivate self-awareness. By participating in an MBSR program, individuals can develop a solid foundation in mindfulness practice and acquire valuable tools for supporting their inner child healing journey.

Visualization

Visualization, the process of creating vivid mental images, can serve as a powerful tool in the realm of inner child healing. By harnessing the power of imagination, individuals can create a safe and comforting mental space in which their inner child can heal and grow. In this section, we will explore the benefits of visualization for inner child healing and discuss various techniques for visualization exercises.

Benefits Of Visualization for Inner Child Healing

Creating a Safe Mental Space

One of the primary benefits of visualization for inner child healing is its ability to create a safe and supportive mental space. By constructing an inner sanctuary, individuals can provide their inner child with a refuge from the harsh realities of the external world. This safe mental space is crucial for fostering emotional healing and resilience, as it enables the inner child to process unresolved emotions and experiences without fear of judgment or criticism.

Enhancing Emotional Connection

Visualization can help individuals forge a deeper emotional connection with their inner child. By regularly visualizing interactions with their inner child, individuals can establish a strong bond and develop a better understanding of their inner child's needs and emotions. This enhanced emotional connection can be invaluable in the healing process, as it enables individuals to provide the love, support, and validation their inner child needs to heal from past wounds.

Facilitating Emotional Release

Visualization can facilitate the release of unresolved childhood emotions by allowing individuals to mentally revisit past experiences and process the emotions associated with them. By doing so, individuals can let go of lingering emotional pain and create space for healing and growth. This emotional release is essential for inner child healing, as it helps individuals break free from the grip of past traumas and move forward with greater emotional resilience.

Reinforcing Positive Change

Visualization can reinforce positive change by helping individuals mentally rehearse new behaviors and emotional responses. By repeatedly visualizing themselves responding to challenging situations with compassion, assertiveness, and emotional intelligence, individuals can gradually rewire their neural pathways and foster lasting change. This reinforcement of positive change is crucial for inner child healing, as it enables individuals to break free from unhealthy patterns and create a more nurturing and supportive environment for their inner child.

Techniques For Visualization Exercises

Inner Child Visualization

Inner child visualization is a powerful technique that can help individuals connect with and nurture their inner child. To practice this visualization, find a quiet and comfortable place to sit or lie down. Close your eyes and take a few deep breaths to relax your body and mind. Then, imagine yourself in a safe and comforting place, such as a serene forest, a tranquil beach, or a cozy room. In this safe space, visualize your inner child, taking note of their appearance, emotions, and body language. Approach your inner child with love and compassion, offering them a warm embrace, soothing words, or any other form of support they may need. You may also choose to engage in a dialogue with your inner child, asking them about their needs, fears, and desires. By regularly practicing this inner child visualization, individuals can develop a deeper emotional connection with their inner child and foster healing and growth.

Safe Space Visualization

Safe space visualization is a technique that can help individuals create a supportive and nurturing environment for their inner child. To practice this visualization, find a quiet and comfortable place to sit or lie down. Close your eyes and take a few deep breaths to relax your body and mind. Then, imagine yourself in a peaceful and soothing environment, such as a lush garden, a tranquil lake, or a cozy cabin. In this safe space, allow yourself to feel completely at ease, protected, and nurtured. As you continue to visualize this safe space, you may choose to invite your inner child to join you, offering them the comfort and security they need to heal and grow. Spend some time in this safe space, exploring it with your inner child and enjoying the feelings of love and support it provides. By regularly practicing this safe space visualization, individuals can create a nurturing environment for their inner child and facilitate emotional healing.

Emotional Release Visualization

Emotional release visualization is a technique that can help individuals process and release unresolved childhood emotions. To practice this visualization, find a quiet and comfortable place to sit or lie down. Close your eyes and take a few deep breaths to relax your body and mind. Then, bring to mind a specific childhood experience or emotion that you wish to address. As you mentally revisit this experience, allow yourself to fully feel the associated emotions without judgment or resistance. Imagine these emotions as energy flowing through and eventually leaving your body. You may also choose to visualize a comforting figure, such as a wise mentor or compassionate friend, offering support and guidance as you process your emotions. By regularly practicing this emotional release visualization, individuals can let go of lingering emotional pain and create space for healing and growth.

Positive Change Visualization

Positive change visualization is a technique that can help individuals reinforce new behaviors and emotional responses. To practice this visualization, find a quiet and comfortable place to sit or lie down. Close your eyes and take a few deep breaths to relax your body and mind. Then, imagine yourself in a challenging situation that typically triggers unhealthy patterns or emotional reactions. As you visualize this situation, imagine yourself responding in a new, healthier way, such as asserting your needs, setting boundaries, or offering yourself compassion and support. As you continue to visualize this positive change, try to fully experience the emotions and sensations associated with this new response. By regularly practicing this positive change visualization, individuals can gradually rewire their neural pathways and foster lasting change in their emotional well-being.

Journaling

Journaling, the practice of regularly writing down one's thoughts, feelings, and experiences, can be a transformative tool in the process of inner child healing. By providing a safe and non-judgmental outlet for self-expression, journaling can help individuals connect with their inner child, process unresolved emotions, and create lasting change. In this section, we will explore the benefits of journaling for inner child healing and discuss various techniques for journaling exercises.

Benefits Of Journaling for Inner Child Healing

Enhancing Self-Awareness

One of the primary benefits of journaling for inner child healing is its ability to enhance self-awareness. By reflecting on their thoughts, feelings, and experiences through writing, individuals can develop a deeper understanding of their inner child's needs, fears, and desires. This increased self-awareness is crucial for inner child healing, as it enables individuals to identify and address the root causes of their emotional pain.

Providing a Safe Outlet for Emotional Expression

Journaling offers a safe and non-judgmental outlet for emotional expression, which can be particularly valuable for individuals working on inner child healing. By allowing themselves to express their feelings freely and without fear of judgment, individuals can create a supportive environment in which their inner child can heal and grow. This emotional expression is essential for processing unresolved emotions and fostering emotional resilience.

Facilitating Emotional Release

Journaling can facilitate the release of unresolved childhood emotions by providing a space for individuals to explore and process their feelings. By writing about their emotions and experiences, individuals can gain insight into the underlying issues contributing to their emotional pain and begin the process of healing. This emotional release is essential for inner child healing, as it helps individuals break free from the grip of past traumas and move forward with greater emotional resilience.

Reinforcing Positive Change

Journaling can reinforce positive change by helping individuals track their progress, set goals, and celebrate their achievements. By regularly documenting their inner child healing journey, individuals can maintain focus on their growth and development and stay motivated to continue making positive changes. This reinforcement of positive change is crucial for inner child healing, as it enables individuals to break free from unhealthy patterns and create a more nurturing and supportive environment for their inner child.

Techniques For Journaling Exercises

Free Writing

Free writing is a journaling technique that involves writing continuously for a set period without concern for grammar, punctuation, or structure. This unfiltered form of self-expression can be particularly valuable for inner child healing, as it enables individuals to connect with their inner child and explore their emotions without judgment or constraint. To practice, free writing, set a timer for a specific amount of time, such as 10 or 20 minutes, and write whatever comes to mind during that time. Allow your thoughts and feelings to flow freely onto the page without worrying about making sense or sounding eloquent. Once the timer goes off, review your writing and reflect on any insights or patterns that may have emerged.

Dialogue with Your Inner Child

Dialogue journaling involves writing a conversation between yourself and your inner child. This journaling technique can help individuals establish a stronger connection with their inner child and gain a better understanding of their needs and emotions. To practice dialogue journaling, begin by writing a question or statement directed at your inner child, such as "How are you feeling today?" or "I'm here to listen and support you." Then, write a response from your inner child's perspective, allowing their voice to come through as authentically as possible. Continue this back-and-forth dialogue for as long as it feels productive and enlightening.

Gratitude Journaling

Gratitude journaling is a technique that involves regularly documenting things for which you are grateful. This practice can be especially beneficial for inner child healing, as it encourages individuals to focus on the positive aspects of their life and cultivate a more optimistic mindset. By regularly expressing gratitude, individuals can create a nurturing and supportive environment for their inner child and foster emotional healing. To practice gratitude journaling, set aside time each day to write down at least three things for which you are grateful. These can be as simple as a warm cup of coffee or as profound as the love and support of a close friend. Over time, this practice can help shift your focus away from negative thoughts and experiences, allowing for greater emotional resilience and inner child healing.

Reflective Journaling

Reflective journaling involves writing about past experiences or situations to gain insight and understanding. This journaling technique can be particularly helpful for inner child healing, as it enables individuals to process unresolved emotions and identify patterns of behavior that may be rooted in childhood experiences. To practice reflective journaling, choose a specific event or situation from your past that you believe may be connected to your inner child's pain. Write a detailed account of the event, including your thoughts, feelings, and reactions at the time. Then, reflect on how this experience may have influenced your current emotions, beliefs, and behaviors, and consider how you can address any lingering issues to foster healing and growth.

Other Techniques

In addition to the previously discussed methods, there are several other techniques that can be beneficial for inner child healing. By incorporating a variety of approaches, individuals can develop a comprehensive and personalized healing plan that addresses their unique needs and circumstances. In this section, we will explore three additional techniques for inner child healing: progressive muscle relaxation, creative expression, and self-compassion exercises.

Progressive Muscle Relaxation

Progressive muscle relaxation (PMR) is a technique that involves tensing and relaxing different muscle groups in the body to promote relaxation and reduce stress. This technique can be particularly helpful for inner child healing, as it enables individuals to release physical tension and create a more relaxed and receptive state for emotional healing. By practicing PMR, individuals can cultivate a greater sense of bodily awareness and develop the ability to regulate their physical and emotional responses to stress.

How to Practice PMR

To practice progressive muscle relaxation, find a quiet and comfortable place to sit or lie down. Close your eyes and take a few deep breaths to relax your body and mind. Beginning with your feet, tense the muscles in your toes and feet for a count of five, then release the tension as you exhale. Move up to your calves, thighs, buttocks, and so on, progressively tensing and relaxing each muscle group until you reach your face and head. As you practice PMR, pay attention to the sensations of tension and relaxation in each muscle group and notice any differences between the two states. By regularly practicing PMR, individuals can develop greater bodily awareness and learn to release physical tension, which can facilitate emotional healing and inner child work.

Creative Expression

Creative expression, such as painting, drawing, dancing, or writing poetry, can be a powerful tool for inner child healing. By engaging in creative activities, individuals can connect with their inner child, explore their emotions, and express themselves in a non-verbal and non-judgmental way. Creative expression can also help individuals develop self-awareness, build self-esteem, and foster a sense of accomplishment and mastery, all of which are essential components of inner child healing.

Creative Expression Exercises for Inner Child Healing

There are countless ways to engage in creative expression for inner child healing. Here are a few ideas to get started:

1. Collage: Create a collage that represents your inner child, using images, words, and colors that resonate with you. This exercise can help you visually explore and express your inner child's feelings, desires, and experiences.

2. Painting or Drawing: Use art materials such as paints, pastels, or colored pencils to create a visual representation of your inner child. This exercise can help you connect with your inner child on a deeper level and provide a safe and non-judgmental outlet for emotional expression.

3. Dance or Movement: Engage in free-form movement or dance to connect with your inner child and express emotions through your body. This exercise can help you release physical tension, build bodily awareness, and cultivate a sense of playfulness and joy.

Self-Compassion Exercises

Self-compassion is the practice of treating oneself with kindness, understanding, and acceptance, especially during times of pain or difficulty. Cultivating self-compassion is essential for inner child healing, as it enables individuals to offer their inner child the love, support, and nurturing they may not have received during childhood. By practicing self-compassion, individuals can develop a more balanced and compassionate perspective on their experiences and emotions, which can facilitate emotional healing and growth.

Self-Compassion Exercises for Inner Child Healing

1. Loving-Kindness Meditation: Loving-kindness meditation is a practice that involves silently repeating phrases of love and goodwill toward oneself and others. To practice loving-kindness meditation for inner child healing, find a quiet and comfortable place to sit or lie down. Close your eyes and begin by focusing on your breath. Next, silently repeat phrases such as "May I be happy, may I be healthy, may I be safe, may I be at ease." As you repeat these phrases, direct your loving-kindness toward your inner child and imagine them receiving this love and compassion. After a few minutes, expand your focus to include other people in your life, such as friends, family, or even strangers. By regularly practicing loving-kindness meditation, individuals can cultivate self-compassion and create a more supportive and nurturing environment for their inner child.

2. Self-Compassionate Letter Writing: Write a letter to your inner child from a compassionate and understanding perspective. In this letter, acknowledge the pain and challenges your inner child has faced and offer words of support, encouragement, and love. This exercise

can help individuals connect with their inner child on a deeper level and cultivate self-compassion.

3. Self-Compassionate Journaling: Practice journaling from a self-compassionate perspective by writing about difficult emotions or experiences in a kind and understanding tone. Rather than judging or criticizing yourself, approach your writing with curiosity, empathy, and compassion. This exercise can help individuals develop a more compassionate and balanced perspective on their emotions and experiences, which can facilitate inner child healing.

Self-Care

Self-care is an essential aspect of the inner child healing process. It involves engaging in activities and practices that promote physical, emotional, and mental well-being. By prioritizing self-care, individuals can create a supportive and nurturing environment that fosters inner child healing and personal growth. In this section, we will discuss the importance of self-care in the inner child healing process and provide practical tips and strategies for incorporating self-care into daily life.

Why Self-Care Matters for Inner Child Healing

Creates a Supportive Environment for Healing

A key component of inner child healing is creating a safe and supportive environment where the inner child can express their needs, emotions, and desires without fear of judgment or criticism. By practicing self-care, individuals can cultivate a sense of safety and security that allows their inner child to heal and grow. Additionally, engaging in self-care practices can help individuals develop a more positive and nurturing relationship with themselves, which is crucial for inner child healing.

Promotes Physical, Emotional, and Mental Well-being

Inner child healing involves addressing unresolved emotional pain and trauma from childhood. This process can be both mentally and emotionally challenging, making it essential for individuals to prioritize their overall well-being. Self-care practices can help individuals maintain physical, emotional, and mental health, enabling them to navigate the healing process more effectively.

Builds Resilience and Coping Skills

The inner child healing process can be a long and difficult journey, requiring individuals to confront and process painful emotions and experiences. By practicing self-care, individuals can build resilience and develop healthy coping skills that support them in managing stress, setbacks, and challenges throughout the healing process.

Enhances Self-Awareness and Personal Growth

Self-care practices can help individuals develop greater self-awareness and insight into their emotions, beliefs, and behaviors. By engaging in self-care, individuals can gain a deeper understanding of their own needs, values, and boundaries, fostering personal growth and healing.

Chapter 5: Overcoming Obstacles to Inner Child Healing

Embarking on the path to inner child healing can be a life-changing experience filled with the potential for deep emotional growth and self-discovery. Yet, it is not without its challenges and obstacles. As individuals delve into their pasts and confront unresolved pain, they may encounter resistance, fear, and other barriers that can make the healing process seem daunting. In Chapter 5, we will explore the various obstacles that one might face on the journey toward inner child healing and provide practical strategies to help overcome these challenges, fostering resilience and perseverance.

The journey of healing the inner child may bring to the surface uncomfortable emotions, hidden fears, and deeply ingrained patterns that can be difficult to navigate. By understanding the common obstacles that individuals face during this process, we can develop a more compassionate and supportive approach to healing. This chapter will delve into topics such as resistance to change, fear of vulnerability, limiting beliefs, the importance of developing a support system, and the role of perseverance and self-compassion in the healing journey.

By shedding light on these challenges and providing guidance on how to address them, we aim to empower individuals to face their inner child healing journey with courage and determination. With the right tools and mindset, it is possible to overcome these obstacles and foster a nurturing environment that facilitates deep and lasting healing. In this chapter, we will equip you with the knowledge and strategies needed to navigate the complexities of inner child healing and continue moving forward on your path toward emotional well-being and self-discovery.

Resistance to Change

Inner child healing is a transformative journey that requires individuals to confront their past and embrace change. However, it is not uncommon for people to encounter resistance during this process. Resistance to change can manifest in various forms and is often rooted in deep-seated fears and beliefs. In this section, we will explore the common reasons for resistance to change and offer strategies for overcoming it, empowering you to move forward in your healing journey.

Common Reasons for Resistance

- Fear of the Unknown: One of the most common reasons for resistance to change is fear of the unknown. Delving into the past and addressing unresolved emotional pain can be unpredictable and unsettling, causing individuals to feel uncertain about the outcome of their healing journey. This fear of the unknown can lead to resistance, as people may prefer to remain in familiar territory, even if it is uncomfortable or harmful.

- Loss of Control: Another common reason for resistance to change is a perceived loss of control. As individuals embark on the inner child healing journey, they may feel that they are surrendering control over their emotions, behaviors, and beliefs. This sense of powerlessness can be distressing and lead to resistance, as people may cling to the illusion of control to avoid feeling vulnerable.

- Comfort in Familiar Patterns: Many individuals find comfort in familiar patterns, even if these patterns are detrimental to their well-being. The process of inner child healing often involves breaking free from these patterns and embracing new ways of thinking, feeling, and behaving. This can be challenging, as it requires individuals to let go of the familiar and embrace the unknown. As a result, resistance may arise as people struggle to release their attachment to familiar patterns.

- Fear of Judgment or Criticism: The journey toward inner child healing often involves confronting painful emotions and experiences that individuals may have kept hidden for years. Fear of judgment or criticism from others, or even from oneself, can lead to resistance to change. Individuals may worry that exploring their past will expose them to ridicule or disapproval, causing them to resist the healing process.

Strategies for Overcoming Resistance

1. Acknowledge and Validate Resistance

The first step in overcoming resistance to change is to acknowledge and validate its presence. Resistance is a natural part of the healing process and serves as an indicator of the challenges one is facing. By recognizing and accepting resistance, individuals can begin to understand its root causes and develop strategies to address them. Validate your feelings of resistance and remind yourself that it is a normal part of the journey toward inner child healing.

2. Cultivate Self-Compassion

Practicing self-compassion can be a powerful tool for overcoming resistance to change. By treating themselves with kindness, understanding, and empathy, individuals can create a safe and supportive environment in which to explore their past and confront their fears. Cultivate self-compassion by acknowledging your feelings, validating your experiences, and offering yourself the same kindness and support you would give to a loved one.

3. Create a Vision of the Desired Outcome

Having a clear vision of the desired outcome can help individuals overcome resistance to change. By visualizing the benefits of inner child healing, such as increased emotional well-being, healthier relationships, and personal growth, individuals can create a sense of motivation and purpose that propels them forward in their healing journey. Spend time reflecting on your goals for inner child healing and envision the person you aspire to become.

4. Develop a Support System

A strong support system can be invaluable in overcoming resistance to change. By surrounding oneself with supportive friends, family members, or professionals, individuals can gain the encouragement and guidance needed to navigate the challenges of the healing process. Reach out to others for support, and consider joining a therapy group or seeking professional assistance from a mental health professional who specializes in inner child healing. By building a network of supportive individuals, you can foster a sense of connection and belonging that will help you face resistance with courage and determination.

5. Break the Process into Manageable Steps

The journey toward inner child healing can sometimes feel overwhelming, leading to resistance to change. One strategy to combat this resistance is to break the process into smaller, manageable steps. By focusing on one aspect of healing at a time, individuals can build confidence and momentum, making the journey less daunting. Create a roadmap for your healing journey, setting attainable goals and celebrating your achievements along the way.

6. Embrace the Learning Process

Resistance to change can often be rooted in fear of making mistakes or failing. By reframing the healing journey as a learning process, individuals can develop a growth mindset that encourages exploration and experimentation. Embrace the learning process by recognizing that setbacks and challenges are opportunities for growth and self-discovery. Remind yourself that inner child healing is a journey, not a destination, and allow yourself the grace to learn and grow at your own pace.

7. Practice Mindfulness

Mindfulness techniques can be effective in overcoming resistance to change, as they encourage individuals to stay present and grounded at the moment. By practicing mindfulness, individuals can develop greater self-awareness and the ability to recognize and address resistance as it arises. Incorporate mindfulness practices, such as meditation or deep breathing exercises, into your daily routine to help cultivate presence and self-awareness during your healing journey.

Fear of Vulnerability

Vulnerability is an integral aspect of the inner child healing process, as it involves opening oneself up to emotions, experiences, and memories that have long been buried or suppressed. Embracing vulnerability can be both empowering and frightening, as it requires individuals to confront their fears, insecurities, and perceived weaknesses. In this section, we will examine the role of vulnerability in inner child healing and provide strategies for overcoming the fear of vulnerability, allowing you to engage in the healing process with courage and authenticity.

The Role of Vulnerability in Inner Child Healing

Emotional Processing and Release

Vulnerability plays a crucial role in inner child healing, as it allows individuals to access and process emotions that have been suppressed or ignored. By embracing vulnerability, individuals can confront their emotional pain, acknowledge its impact on their lives, and release it, creating space for healing and growth.

Authenticity and Self-Awareness

Opening oneself up to vulnerability fosters a sense of authenticity and self-awareness. By confronting and accepting one's emotional experiences, individuals can develop a deeper understanding of themselves and their needs, allowing them to cultivate a more genuine and honest relationship with themselves and others.

Connection and Empathy

Vulnerability is the foundation of emotional connection and empathy. By embracing vulnerability, individuals can build stronger, more authentic connections with others, as they are able to share their experiences, emotions, and struggles openly and honestly. This sense of connection and empathy can be a powerful catalyst for healing, as it fosters a supportive environment in which individuals can explore their past and confront their emotional pain.

Strategies for Overcoming Fear of Vulnerability

Recognize and Challenge Fear-Based Beliefs

One of the first steps in overcoming the fear of vulnerability is to recognize and challenge the fear-based beliefs that often underlie it. These beliefs may include ideas that vulnerability is a sign of weakness, that expressing emotions is dangerous, or that one must maintain a facade of strength and independence at all times. By identifying and challenging these beliefs, individuals can begin to reshape their perspective on vulnerability, embracing it as a source of strength and healing.

Practice Self-Compassion

As with resistance to change, self-compassion is a valuable tool in overcoming the fear of vulnerability. By treating oneself with kindness, understanding, and empathy, individuals can create a safe space in which to explore their emotions and experiences without fear of judgment or rejection. Cultivate self-compassion by acknowledging your fears, validating your emotions, and offering yourself the same care and support you would extend to a loved one.

Develop a Support System

A strong support system can be instrumental in overcoming the fear of vulnerability. Surrounding oneself with supportive and understanding friends, family members, or professionals can help individuals feel safe and secure as they navigate the challenges of inner child healing. Seek out individuals who are empathetic, non-judgmental, and willing to listen, and consider joining a support group or working with a therapist who specializes in inner child healing.

Take Small Steps Towards Vulnerability

Overcoming the fear of vulnerability is often a gradual process that involves taking small, manageable steps toward embracing emotional openness. Begin by practicing vulnerability in low-risk situations, such as sharing your thoughts or feelings with a trusted friend or journaling about your emotions. As you become more comfortable with vulnerability, gradually increase the level of emotional risk, eventually incorporating vulnerability into more challenging aspects of your healing journey.

Use Mindfulness Techniques

Mindfulness techniques can help individuals overcome the fear of vulnerability by encouraging them to stay present and grounded at the moment. Through mindfulness practices, such as meditation or deep breathing exercises, individuals can develop the ability to remain present with their emotions, even when they feel overwhelmed or frightened. Cultivating mindfulness can also help individuals recognize and manage the physical symptoms of fear and anxiety that often accompany vulnerability, allowing them to approach the healing process with greater calm and confidence.

Reframe Vulnerability as Strength

One powerful strategy for overcoming the fear of vulnerability is to reframe it as a sign of strength and courage rather than weakness or failure. By choosing to embrace vulnerability and confront one's emotional pain, individuals demonstrate immense bravery and resilience. Acknowledge the strength and courage it takes to face your fears and delve into your emotional wounds, and remind yourself that vulnerability is a testament to your determination and commitment to healing.

Finally, it can be helpful to remind oneself of the transformative potential of vulnerability in the inner child healing process. By embracing vulnerability, individuals can access deep emotional reservoirs, foster authentic connections with others, and cultivate a greater sense of self-awareness and personal growth. Recognize that vulnerability is not only an essential aspect of inner child healing but also a powerful catalyst for personal transformation and growth.

Limiting Beliefs

Limiting beliefs are deeply ingrained assumptions or convictions that often hold individuals back from realizing their full potential and achieving their goals. These beliefs can be particularly detrimental to the inner child healing process, as they can prevent individuals from embracing vulnerability, confronting emotional pain, and moving forward on their healing journey. In this section, we will explore how to identify limiting beliefs and provide strategies for challenging and changing these beliefs to support the inner child healing process.

Identifying Limiting Beliefs

- Explore Your Thought Patterns: To identify limiting beliefs, begin by paying close attention to your thought patterns and the way you talk to yourself. Limiting beliefs often manifest as negative self-talk, such as thoughts like "I'm not good enough," "I can't handle this," or "I don't deserve happiness." By becoming aware of these thoughts and examining their origins, you can begin to uncover the limiting beliefs that underlie them.

- Reflect on Past Experiences: Another effective way to identify limiting beliefs is to reflect on your past experiences and consider how they may have shaped your beliefs about yourself, others, and the world around you. For example, if you experienced a traumatic event in your childhood, you may have developed limiting beliefs around trust, self-worth, or your ability to form healthy relationships. By exploring these experiences and their impact on your belief system, you can gain insight into the limiting beliefs that may be holding you back in your healing journey.

- Examine Your Emotional Reactions: Limiting beliefs can also be identified by examining your emotional reactions to certain situations or triggers. If you find yourself feeling anxious, fearful, or defensive in response to specific circumstances, consider the beliefs that may be driving these emotions. For example, if you become extremely anxious when faced with the prospect of opening up to others, you may hold a limiting belief that vulnerability is dangerous or that others will judge or reject you if they know your true feelings.

Challenging and Changing Limiting Beliefs

Question the Validity of Your Beliefs

Once you have identified your limiting beliefs, the first step in challenging and changing them is to question their validity. Ask yourself whether these beliefs are rooted in objective facts or whether they are based on subjective interpretations, assumptions, or fears. By examining the evidence for and against your limiting beliefs, you can begin to weaken their hold on your thoughts and behaviors.

Consider Alternative Perspectives

Another effective strategy for challenging and changing limiting beliefs is to consider alternative perspectives and interpretations. For example, if you hold the belief that you are unworthy of love, consider the possibility that your past experiences have led you to develop this belief but that it does not reflect your inherent worth as a person. By exploring alternative viewpoints and challenging the assumptions underlying your limiting beliefs, you can create space for new, more empowering beliefs to take their place.

Reframe Your Limiting Beliefs

Reframing your limiting beliefs involves changing the way you think about and interpret your experiences, emotions, and behaviors. Instead of viewing your limiting beliefs as unchangeable truths, consider them as hypotheses that can be tested and modified. By adopting a more flexible and open-minded approach to your belief system, you can begin to reshape your thoughts and behaviors in a way that supports your healing journey.

Use Cognitive-Behavioral Techniques

Cognitive-behavioral techniques can be highly effective in challenging and changing limiting beliefs, as they involve identifying and modifying negative thought patterns and behaviors. Techniques such as thought restructuring, cognitive restructuring, and exposure therapy can help individuals confront and change their limiting beliefs, allowing them to develop a more adaptive and supportive belief system.

Practice Self-Compassion

As with other aspects of inner child healing, practicing self-compassion is a crucial element in challenging and changing limiting beliefs. By cultivating kindness and understanding towards yourself, you can begin to challenge the negative self-talk and beliefs that contribute to your emotional pain. When you encounter a limiting belief, remind yourself that you are human and that it is natural to have fears and insecurities. Instead of criticizing yourself for holding these beliefs, approach them with curiosity and a desire to understand their origins.

Seek Professional Support

If you find it difficult to challenge and change your limiting beliefs on your own, consider seeking the support of a mental health professional, such as a therapist or counselor. These professionals can help you explore the root causes of your limiting beliefs and provide guidance on how to challenge and change them effectively. Additionally, they can offer support and encouragement as you navigate the often difficult and emotional process of inner child healing.

Surround Yourself with Positive Influences

The people and environments that surround us can have a significant impact on our belief systems. To facilitate the process of challenging and changing limiting beliefs, surround yourself with positive influences that encourage personal growth, self-reflection, and emotional healing. Engage in activities and relationships that foster a sense of self-worth, belonging, and empowerment, and seek out individuals who inspire you to challenge your limiting beliefs and embrace your true potential.

Developing a Support System

A strong support system is crucial to the process of inner child healing. Social support can provide emotional comfort, encouragement, and practical assistance as individuals navigate the often challenging journey toward emotional healing and personal growth. In this section, we will discuss the importance of social support in inner child healing and provide strategies for building a support system that can facilitate this transformative journey.

The Importance of Social Support in Inner Child Healing

- Emotional Comfort and Validation: One of the most significant benefits of social support is the emotional comfort and validation it provides. As individuals work to heal their inner child, they may experience a range of difficult emotions, including sadness, anger, fear, and shame. A supportive network of friends, family members, or therapists can provide a safe space for individuals to express these emotions without fear of judgment or rejection. This emotional validation can be essential in helping individuals process and make sense of their experiences, ultimately fostering emotional healing and growth.

- Encouragement and Motivation: Healing the inner child is a long and often arduous process that requires determination, persistence, and courage. A strong support system can provide encouragement and motivation, helping individuals stay committed to their healing journey even in the face of setbacks and obstacles. By offering words of affirmation, sharing personal stories of growth, and celebrating accomplishments, a support network can help individuals maintain their resolve and focus on their personal growth and healing.

- Practical Assistance: In addition to providing emotional comfort and encouragement, a support system can also offer practical assistance in the form of resources, guidance, and advice. For example, friends and family members can help individuals research therapy options, attend support groups, or develop self-care routines. This practical assistance can help individuals overcome barriers to healing and ensure they have the tools and resources necessary to facilitate their inner child healing process.

Strategies for Building a Support System

Cultivate Existing Relationships

One of the most effective ways to build a support system is by cultivating and strengthening existing relationships. Reach out to friends, family members, or colleagues who have demonstrated empathy, understanding, and support in the past. Share your healing journey with these individuals, and express your desire for their continued support and encouragement. By fostering open communication and trust in your existing relationships, you can create a solid foundation for your support system.

Seek Professional Support

Professional support, such as therapy or counseling, can be an invaluable component of a support system for inner child healing. Mental health professionals have specialized training and expertise in helping individuals navigate the emotional complexities of healing and personal growth. They can provide guidance, support, and evidence-based interventions tailored to your unique needs and circumstances. To find a therapist or counselor who specializes in inner child healing, consider conducting online research, asking for recommendations from friends or family members, or contacting your local mental health clinic.

Join Support Groups or Communities

Support groups and communities can offer a sense of connection, understanding, and shared experience that can be incredibly valuable in the healing process. By joining a support group or community, you can connect with others who are also working to heal their inner child, share your experiences and insights, and gain inspiration from the collective wisdom of the group. Look for support groups or communities in your local area or online that focus on topics related to inner child healing, such as trauma recovery, self-compassion, or personal growth.

Practice Vulnerability

Building a support system often requires vulnerability, as it involves opening up about your experiences, emotions, and needs. While vulnerability can be frightening, it is also a powerful catalyst for connection and healing. Practice vulnerability by sharing your thoughts, feelings, and experiences with those you trust, and be open to receiving support and encouragement in return. As you become more comfortable with vulnerability, you may find that your support system naturally grows and strengthens.

Set Boundaries

While building a support system is important, it is also essential to set boundaries with the people in your life. Establishing healthy boundaries can help protect your emotional well-being, prevent burnout, and ensure that your relationships remain supportive and balanced. Communicate your needs and limits clearly, and be willing to enforce those boundaries when necessary. Remember that a strong support system is built on mutual respect and understanding, and setting boundaries is an essential aspect of maintaining those qualities in your relationships.

Be Supportive of Others

One of the most effective ways to build a support system is by being a supportive friend, family member, or partner yourself. Offer encouragement, understanding, and empathy to those around you, and be willing to lend a listening ear or a helping hand when needed. By fostering a supportive and compassionate environment in your relationships, you are more likely to attract like-minded individuals who can reciprocate that support and contribute to your healing journey.

Cultivate a Diverse Support System

A diverse support system can provide a range of perspectives, experiences, and resources that can be invaluable in the inner child healing process. Seek out connections with individuals from various backgrounds, age groups, and life experiences to create a support network that can offer a wide range of insights and guidance. Remember that each person in your support system can bring unique strengths and contributions to your healing journey, and by cultivating a diverse network, you can ensure that you have access to a broad range of support and resources.

Perseverance and Self-Compassion

Perseverance and self-compassion are two critical components of the inner child healing journey. Both qualities play a vital role in fostering emotional growth and recovery, and they are essential for overcoming the obstacles and challenges that often arise during the process of healing. In this section, we will explore the importance of perseverance and self-compassion in the inner child healing journey and discuss strategies for cultivating these qualities within ourselves.

Perseverance: The Key to Progress

Embrace the Process

Healing your inner child is a complex and often lengthy journey, requiring patience, commitment, and resilience. It is important to recognize that progress may be slow and that setbacks are a natural part of the healing process. Embrace the journey as an opportunity for growth and self-discovery, and be prepared to face the challenges and obstacles that may arise along the way.

Stay Focused on Your Goals

Keeping your goals in mind is crucial for maintaining perseverance throughout the healing journey. Remind yourself regularly of the reasons behind your decision to embark on the path of inner child healing, and focus on the benefits and improvements you hope to achieve. By staying focused on your goals and aspirations, you can maintain the motivation and determination needed to overcome the challenges and setbacks that may arise.

Be Adaptable

Adaptability is an essential quality for persevering in the face of obstacles and setbacks. Be open to modifying your approach, exploring new strategies, and adjusting your expectations as needed. Recognize that healing is an evolving process and that your path may shift and change as you grow and learn. By remaining flexible and adaptable, you can better navigate the challenges that may arise during your healing journey.

Self-Compassion: The Power of Self-Kindness

Cultivate Self-Awareness

Developing self-compassion begins with cultivating self-awareness. This involves recognizing your own thoughts, feelings, and experiences and acknowledging the pain and suffering that may be present within you. By becoming more attuned to your own emotional landscape, you can better understand and empathize with your own struggles and challenges.

Offer Yourself Kindness and Understanding

Once you have developed a greater awareness of your own emotional experiences, it is essential to extend kindness and understanding toward yourself. Treat yourself with the same care, compassion, and patience that you would offer to a close friend or family member who is struggling. Recognize that everyone experiences challenges and setbacks and that you deserve kindness and support as you navigate your own healing journey.

Challenge Negative Self-Talk

Negative self-talk is a common obstacle to self-compassion, as it often reinforces feelings of unworthiness, shame, and self-blame. To cultivate self-compassion, it is important to challenge and reframe these negative thought patterns. When you catch yourself engaging in negative self-talk, pause and ask yourself whether you would speak to a loved one in the same way. If not, consider how you can reframe your thoughts in a more compassionate and supportive manner.

Practice Mindfulness

Mindfulness is a powerful tool for cultivating self-compassion, as it encourages non-judgmental awareness and acceptance of our thoughts and feelings. By practicing mindfulness, we can develop a greater understanding of our own emotional experiences and learn to respond to our own pain and suffering with kindness and empathy.

Create a Self-Compassion Ritual

Developing a self-compassion ritual can be a helpful strategy for nurturing self-compassion on a regular basis. This might involve setting aside time each day or week to engage in activities that promote self-kindness and understanding, such as journaling, meditation, or engaging in self-care practices. By making self-compassion a consistent part of your routine, you can reinforce the importance of self-kindness and empathy in your healing journey.

Surround Yourself with Compassionate Influences

The people and environments you surround yourself with can significantly impact your ability to cultivate self-compassion. Seek out supportive, compassionate individuals who can offer understanding and empathy as you navigate your healing journey. Additionally, immerse yourself in books, podcasts, or other resources that promote self-compassion and emotional well-being.

Acknowledge and Celebrate Your Progress

It is essential to recognize and celebrate your progress as you work towards healing your inner child. Acknowledge the effort and determination you have invested in your journey, and take time to appreciate the growth and transformation you have experienced. Celebrating your progress can help to reinforce the importance of perseverance and self-compassion and motivate you to continue moving forward in your healing journey.

Chapter 6: Healing Relationships through Inner Child Work

Healing relationships through inner child work can be transformative, as it addresses the root of many issues that affect our adult relationships. By understanding and healing our childhood wounds, we can improve the way we relate to ourselves and others, fostering healthier connections that are grounded in love, trust, and understanding. In this chapter, we will discuss the impact of childhood wounds on adult relationships, identify relationship patterns related to these wounds, and explore strategies for addressing these patterns through inner child work. Furthermore, we will emphasize the importance of communication and boundary-setting in maintaining healthy relationships.

Childhood Wounds and Relationships

The experiences we have during our formative years play a crucial role in shaping our personalities, beliefs, and behaviors in adulthood. Childhood wounds, such as emotional, physical, or sexual abuse, neglect, or witnessing violence or conflict, can leave deep emotional scars that persist well into adulthood. These unresolved issues can significantly impact our adult relationships, leading to a range of emotional, psychological, and behavioral challenges.

The impact of childhood wounds on adult relationships can manifest in various ways. Some of the most common effects include the following:

- Difficulty forming and maintaining healthy relationships: Individuals who experience childhood wounds may struggle to develop and maintain meaningful connections with others. This could be due to a fear of vulnerability, a lack of trust, or low self-esteem. These challenges can lead to isolation and loneliness, further exacerbating emotional distress.

- Repeating unhealthy relationship patterns: Childhood wounds often lead to the formation of unhealthy relationship patterns in adulthood. For example, a person who experienced emotional neglect as a child may be drawn to emotionally unavailable partners or engage in self-sabotaging behaviors in relationships. These patterns can be difficult to break without addressing the underlying childhood wounds.

- Emotional dysregulation: Childhood trauma can hinder the development of healthy emotional regulation skills, making it challenging for individuals to manage their emotions effectively. This can lead to increased emotional reactivity, intense mood swings, and difficulty coping with stress and conflict in relationships.

- Attachment issues: Childhood wounds can disrupt the development of secure attachment, leading to attachment issues in adulthood. These issues can manifest as an anxious attachment (clinginess, fear of abandonment) or avoidant attachment (emotional distance, fear of intimacy), both of which can negatively impact relationships.

- Trust issues: Experiencing betrayal, abuse, or neglect during childhood can significantly damage an individual's ability to trust others. This lack of trust can create barriers to intimacy and vulnerability in relationships, making it difficult to form deep, meaningful connections.

Identifying Relationship Patterns Related to Childhood Wounds

Recognizing and understanding the relationship patterns that stem from childhood wounds is the first step in addressing and transforming them. To identify these patterns, consider the following strategies:

- Reflect on past relationships: Take some time to think about your previous relationships and identify any recurring patterns or themes. Consider how these patterns may be connected to your childhood experiences. For example, if you consistently find yourself in relationships with emotionally unavailable partners, this could be a reflection of unmet emotional needs during childhood.

- Examine your beliefs about relationships: Our beliefs about relationships often stem from our early experiences with our caregivers. Reflect on the messages you received about love, trust, and intimacy growing up, and consider how these beliefs might be influencing your current relationship patterns. For instance, if you were raised to believe that love is conditional, you might struggle with feelings of unworthiness and have difficulty accepting love and affection from others.

- Explore your attachment style: Understanding your attachment style can provide valuable insights into your relationship patterns and the childhood wounds that may be contributing to them. If you identify with an anxious or avoidant attachment style, consider exploring the childhood experiences that may have contributed to this development.

- Notice emotional triggers: Emotional triggers can provide important clues about the childhood wounds that are influencing your relationships. Pay attention to the situations or experiences that provoke strong emotional reactions in you, and consider how these triggers might be connected to past traumas or unmet needs.

- Seek professional support: A therapist or counselor experienced in working with childhood wounds and relationship issues can help you identify and understand the patterns that are impacting your relationships. They can also provide guidance and support as you work towards healing and transforming these patterns.

Addressing Relationship Patterns

Addressing and transforming the relationship patterns rooted in childhood wounds is essential for fostering healthy, fulfilling relationships in adulthood. Inner child work can be a powerful tool for healing these patterns by helping individuals identify, understand, and process the childhood experiences that are impacting their adult relationships. Here are some strategies for addressing relationship patterns through inner child work:

- Identify your inner child's needs: Understanding the unmet needs of your inner child is crucial for healing and transforming relationship patterns. Reflect on the experiences and emotions from your childhood and consider what needs were not met or acknowledged. These needs may include safety, love, acceptance, or validation.

- Establish a connection with your inner child: Developing a compassionate, nurturing relationship with your inner child is key to the healing process. You can establish this connection through techniques such as visualization, journaling, or mindfulness. By connecting with your inner child, you can better understand their experiences, emotions, and needs, which can provide valuable insights into your relationship patterns.

- Validate and comfort your inner child: One of the primary goals of inner child work is to provide the love, validation, and comfort that your inner child may not have received in childhood. Practice validating your inner child's feelings and experiences and offer comfort and reassurance. This process can help to heal emotional wounds and create a more secure foundation for your adult relationships.

- Reparenting your inner child: Reparenting involves providing the guidance, support, and nurturing that your inner child may have missed out on during childhood. This can include setting healthy boundaries, encouraging self-care, and promoting emotional regulation. By reparenting your inner child, you can help to create new, healthier relationship patterns in your adult life.

- Address and challenge limiting beliefs: Limiting beliefs that stem from childhood wounds can perpetuate unhealthy relationship patterns. Identify and challenge these beliefs by questioning their validity and replacing them with more empowering, supportive beliefs. This process can help to shift your mindset and pave the way for healthier relationships.

- Seek professional support: A therapist or counselor experienced in inner child work can provide valuable guidance and support as you address and transform your relationship patterns. They can help you navigate the healing process and develop the skills needed to cultivate healthy, fulfilling relationships in adulthood.

The Importance of Communication and Boundary-Setting in Healthy Relationships

Effective communication and boundary-setting are essential components of healthy relationships. These skills can help to foster trust, respect, and emotional intimacy while preventing misunderstandings and conflicts. Here are some reasons why communication and boundary-setting are crucial for maintaining healthy relationships:

1. Clarity and understanding: Clear communication helps to ensure that both partners in a relationship understand each other's needs, feelings, and perspectives. This understanding can prevent misunderstandings and misinterpretations that can lead to conflict and emotional distance.

2. Emotional expression: Open, honest communication allows both partners to express their emotions freely and without fear of judgment or rejection. This emotional expression can foster emotional intimacy and create a strong foundation for a healthy relationship.

3. Conflict resolution: Effective communication is crucial for resolving conflicts and disagreements in a respectful and constructive manner. By discussing issues openly and honestly, partners can work together to find solutions and compromises that meet both of their needs.

4. Boundary-setting: Establishing and maintaining healthy boundaries is essential for preserving the emotional well-being and autonomy of both partners in a relationship. Boundaries can include physical, emotional, and mental limits, and they help to create a sense of safety and respect within the relationship.

5. Trust and respect: Clear communication and boundary-setting can help to build trust and respect in a relationship. When both partners feel heard, understood, and respected, they are more likely to trust each other and invest in the relationship.

6. Personal growth and development: Effective communication and boundary-setting can contribute to personal growth and development within a relationship. By expressing needs and desires, individuals can learn more about themselves, their partners, and the relationship dynamics. This growth can lead to a deeper understanding of each other and a stronger, more resilient partnership.

To enhance communication and boundary-setting skills in your relationships, consider the following strategies:

- Practice active listening: Active listening involves fully engaging in what your partner is saying without interrupting or formulating a response. This attentiveness can help to create an open, supportive environment for communication and foster a sense of understanding and empathy.

- Use "I" statements: Expressing your thoughts and feelings using "I" statements can help to create a non-confrontational tone and reduce defensiveness in your partner. For example, instead of saying, "You never listen to me," try saying, "I feel unheard when I share my thoughts with you."

- Be assertive: Assertive communication involves expressing your needs, feelings and desires directly and respectfully. Practice being assertive by clearly stating your needs and setting boundaries without aggression or passivity.

- Develop emotional awareness: Understanding and managing your emotions is crucial for effective communication. Develop your emotional awareness by practicing mindfulness, journaling, or engaging in therapy or counseling.

- Establish and maintain boundaries: Clearly define your personal boundaries and communicate them to your partner. Be consistent in enforcing these boundaries and respect your partner's boundaries as well.

- Seek support: If you struggle with communication and boundary-setting, consider seeking support from a therapist, counselor, or support group. These professionals and communities can provide guidance and resources to help you develop these essential relationship skills.

Chapter 7: Addressing Abandonment Wounds through Inner Child Work

Embarking on a journey of self-discovery and healing is a transformative experience, especially when confronting the deep-seated wounds from childhood. One particularly painful and challenging wound to address is the abandonment wound, which can have lasting effects on our self-esteem, relationships, and overall emotional wellbeing. In this chapter, we will explore the complex issue of abandonment wounds and offer valuable tools and strategies for working through these painful experiences using inner child work.

Abandonment wounds can manifest in various ways and stem from multiple sources, including parental divorce, death, emotional neglect, or any experience that leaves an individual feeling rejected, unloved, or unworthy. These wounds can have a significant impact on one's sense of self and can shape patterns of behavior, thought, and emotion that persists into adulthood.

As we delve into the intricacies of abandonment wounds, we will discuss common signs and symptoms that may indicate the presence of these deeply rooted emotional scars. Furthermore, we will explore the potential consequences of abandonment wounds and the ways they can influence adult relationships, self-esteem, and emotional regulation.

Armed with a greater understanding of abandonment wounds, we will then present various strategies for addressing and healing these wounds through inner child work. By adapting Cognitive-Behavioral Therapy (CBT) techniques and incorporating additional therapeutic approaches, we will provide you with a comprehensive toolkit for working through your abandonment wounds and fostering emotional healing.

This chapter aims to empower you with the knowledge and resources to embark on a journey of self-discovery, healing, and transformation. By addressing your abandonment wounds, you will be better equipped to cultivate healthier relationships, improve emotional regulation, and nurture a strong, resilient sense of self.

Identifying Abandonment Wounds

Abandonment wounds are deep emotional scars that often develop during childhood and can persist into adulthood, affecting individuals' emotional wellbeing and their relationships. Understanding and identifying abandonment wounds is essential for embarking on a journey of self-discovery, growth, and healing. In this section, we will explore the common signs of abandonment wounds and the significant impact they can have on various aspects of one's life.

Common Signs of Abandonment Wounds

Fear of Rejection intense fear of rejection, constantly worrying that others will leave or reject them. This fear can manifest as clinginess, jealousy, or an excessive need for reassurance in relationships.

- Trust Issues: Those who have experienced abandonment in their past may struggle to trust others, often questioning their loved ones' loyalty and fearing betrayal. This lack of trust can create barriers to forming deep, meaningful connections with others.

- Difficulty with Emotional Intimacy: Abandonment wounds can lead to difficulties with emotional intimacy, as individuals may be hesitant to open up and share their feelings with others. They may fear that vulnerability will lead to further rejection or abandonment.

- Low Self-Esteem: Abandonment can leave individuals feeling unworthy, unlovable, or defective in some way. This can result in low self-esteem and a negative self-image, which can impact various aspects of their life, including relationships, careers, and mental health.

- Chronic Loneliness: Individuals with abandonment wounds may feel a persistent sense of loneliness, even when surrounded by friends and loved ones. This feeling of isolation can stem from a deep-seated belief that they are fundamentally unlovable or unworthy of connection.

- Emotional Dysregulation: Abandonment wounds can lead to difficulty managing and expressing emotions, resulting in emotional outbursts, mood swings, or a tendency to suppress emotions altogether.

- Codependency: As a coping mechanism, those with abandonment wounds may develop codependent tendencies, becoming overly reliant on their partner or loved ones for emotional support, validation, and a sense of security.

- Self-Sabotaging Behaviors: To protect themselves from the perceived threat of abandonment, individuals may engage in self-sabotaging behaviors, such as pushing people away, creating unnecessary conflicts, or undermining their own success.

The Impact of Abandonment Wounds

Abandonment wounds can have a far-reaching impact on an individual's life, affecting their emotional wellbeing, relationships, and overall functioning.

- Emotional Wellbeing: The emotional pain and turmoil associated with abandonment wounds can lead to anxiety, depression, and other mental health challenges. The constant fear of rejection or abandonment can create a pervasive sense of unease and dissatisfaction, preventing individuals from experiencing true emotional fulfillment.

- Relationships: Abandonment wounds can significantly impact romantic, familial, and platonic relationships. The fear of rejection, trust issues, and difficulty with emotional intimacy can lead to a pattern of unstable or unhealthy relationships. Individuals may find themselves drawn to unavailable partners, perpetuating the cycle of abandonment and reinforcing their negative self-beliefs.

- Career and Success: Low self-esteem and self-sabotaging behaviors can hinder an individual's ability to achieve success in their career or other pursuits. They may struggle with self-confidence, procrastination, or self-doubt, preventing them from realizing their full potential.

- Emotional Resilience: Abandonment wounds can undermine an individual's emotional resilience, making it more challenging to cope with stress, adversity, or other life challenges. The lack of a secure emotional foundation can exacerbate feelings of helplessness and vulnerability during difficult times.

- Sense of Identity: The negative self-beliefs that often accompany abandonment wounds can impact an individual's sense of identity, leading to confusion or uncertainty about who they truly are and what they want in life. This lack of self-awareness can hinder personal growth and make it difficult for individuals to form authentic connections with others.

Strategies for Addressing Abandonment Wounds

Healing from abandonment wounds can be a challenging but rewarding journey. It requires dedication, self-awareness, and the willingness to face painful emotions head-on. There are various strategies and techniques that can help individuals address their abandonment wounds, leading to a more fulfilling and emotionally healthy life. In this section, we will discuss adapting Cognitive Behavioral Therapy (CBT) for abandonment wounds and explore other techniques for addressing these deep emotional scars.

Adapting CBT for Abandonment Wounds

- Cognitive Behavioral Therapy (CBT) is an evidence-based psychological treatment that focuses on identifying and modifying negative thought patterns and behaviors. It has been successfully used to treat a wide range of emotional issues, including anxiety, depression, and trauma-related disorders. Adapting CBT for abandonment wounds involves using its principles and techniques to specifically address the negative beliefs, thought patterns, and behaviors associated with these emotional scars.

- Identifying Negative Thoughts and Beliefs: The first step in using CBT for abandonment wounds is to identify the negative thoughts and beliefs that stem from the experience of abandonment. This may include beliefs such as "I am unlovable," "No one will ever stay," or "I must be perfect to be accepted." By recognizing these thoughts, individuals can begin to challenge and change them.

- Challenging Negative Thoughts: Once negative thoughts have been identified, individuals can use CBT techniques to challenge and reframe them. This may involve examining the evidence for and against the thought, looking for alternative explanations, or exploring the worst-case scenario. Challenging negative thoughts helps individuals develop a more balanced and accurate perspective on their experiences and emotions.

- Changing Behaviors: Abandonment wounds often result in maladaptive behaviors, such as clinging to relationships, avoiding emotional intimacy, or engaging in self-sabotage. Using CBT, individuals can identify these behaviors and work on replacing them with healthier alternatives. This may involve setting boundaries, improving communication skills, or learning to cope with emotions more effectively.

- Emotion Regulation: CBT can also be used to help individuals develop better emotion regulation skills. This may involve teaching techniques such as mindfulness, progressive muscle relaxation, or cognitive restructuring to manage intense emotions and prevent emotional outbursts or impulsive actions.

- Building Self-Esteem: A crucial aspect of healing from abandonment wounds is rebuilding self-esteem. CBT can help individuals identify and challenge the negative self-beliefs that contribute to low self-esteem, replacing them with more positive and accurate beliefs about themselves.

Other Techniques for Addressing Abandonment Wounds

In addition to CBT, there are several other techniques that can be effective in addressing abandonment wounds. These approaches can be used in conjunction with CBT or as standalone strategies, depending on individual needs and preferences.

- Inner Child Work: As mentioned in previous chapters, inner child work is a powerful technique for addressing deep emotional wounds, including abandonment. This approach involves connecting with the hurt, vulnerable child within and providing the love, support, and validation that may have been missing in childhood.

- Mindfulness and Meditation: Mindfulness and meditation practices can be highly beneficial in addressing abandonment wounds. These techniques promote self-awareness, emotional regulation, and self-compassion, which can help individuals recognize and heal the emotional pain associated with abandonment.

- EMDR (Eye Movement Desensitization and Reprocessing): EMDR is a trauma-focused therapy that has been found to be effective in treating various emotional issues, including abandonment wounds. This technique involves using bilateral stimulation (such as eye movements or tapping) while recalling traumatic memories, helping individuals process and release the emotional pain associated with the experience.

- Attachment-Based Therapy: Attachment-based therapies focus on the underlying attachment issues that often contribute to abandonment wounds. By exploring early attachment experiences and addressing the resulting patterns, individuals can develop healthier attachment styles and improve their relationships. This approach may involve working with a therapist who specializes in attachment theory or engaging in couples therapy to address attachment issues within a relationship.

- Expressive Arts Therapy: Creative outlets such as art, music, dance, or writing can be therapeutic in addressing abandonment wounds. Expressive arts therapy encourages individuals to use creative expression as a means of processing and emotionally healing pain. This approach can be particularly helpful for those who struggle to articulate their feelings or find traditional talk therapy challenging.

- Support Groups: Joining a support group for individuals who have experienced abandonment can provide a safe space for sharing experiences, learning from others, and receiving validation and encouragement. Support groups can be found in-person or online and can be an invaluable resource for healing and personal growth.

- Self-Care and Self-Compassion: Practicing self-care and self-compassion is essential for healing from abandonment wounds. This involves taking care of one's physical, emotional, and mental wellbeing and learning to treat oneself with kindness and understanding. Self-compassion practices may include positive affirmations, self-soothing techniques, or engaging in activities that bring joy and relaxation.

- Professional Help: Seeking professional help from a therapist or counselor experienced in abandonment issues can be beneficial in addressing the complex emotions and patterns associated with these wounds. A skilled professional can provide guidance, support, and tailored interventions to help individuals work through their abandonment issues and develop healthier coping strategies.

Chapter 8: Addressing Neglect Wounds through Inner Child Work

Chapter 8 of "Healing Your Inner Child: Cognitive Behavioral Therapy Strategies to Address Trauma and Abandonment Wounds" focuses on the topic of neglect wounds and how to address them through inner child work. Neglect is a form of childhood trauma that occurs when a caregiver fails to provide adequate care or attention to a child's physical, emotional, or psychological needs. This can have significant impacts on an individual's emotional and psychological well-being, making it important to identify and address these wounds.

The chapter begins by exploring the common signs of neglect wounds. These signs can manifest in a range of emotional and behavioral ways, including low self-esteem, anxiety, depression, difficulty with trust, difficulty with emotional regulation, difficulty forming healthy relationships, substance abuse, lack of self-care, and difficulty setting boundaries. Understanding these signs can help readers identify if they or someone they know may be experiencing neglect wounds.

The chapter then delves into the impact of neglect wounds on a person's life. Neglect wounds can lead to a lack of self-esteem and confidence, making it difficult to form healthy relationships and regulate emotions. These wounds can impact a person's sense of self-worth and lead to negative beliefs about oneself. By understanding the impact of neglect wounds, readers can begin to see the importance of addressing these wounds and moving towards healing and growth.

The chapter then provides strategies for addressing neglect wounds through inner child work. The first strategy discussed is adapting cognitive-behavioral therapy (CBT) techniques for neglect wounds. CBT focuses on identifying negative thought patterns and replacing them with positive ones. For individuals with neglect wounds, this may involve identifying and challenging negative self-talk and developing positive coping mechanisms for managing emotions. The chapter also discusses other techniques for addressing neglect wounds, including mindfulness, art therapy, and group therapy.

By the end of the chapter, readers will have a deeper understanding of how to identify neglect wounds and the impact they can have on adult life. They will also have a range of strategies for addressing these wounds through inner child work, including adapting CBT techniques and exploring other therapeutic approaches. By working through these strategies, readers can move towards healing from the effects of neglect and find a sense of inner peace and self-love.

Identifying Neglect Wounds

Neglect is a form of childhood trauma that occurs when a caregiver fails to provide adequate care or attention to a child's physical, emotional, or psychological needs. Neglect wounds can be difficult to identify, but it is important to recognize the common signs and understand their impact on a person's emotional and psychological well-being.

Common Signs of Neglect Wounds

Neglect wounds can manifest in a range of emotional and behavioral signs. It is important to recognize these signs so that individuals can begin to identify if they or someone they know may be experiencing neglect wounds. Some common signs of neglect wounds include:

- Low self-esteem: Individuals who have experienced neglect wounds may struggle with feelings of low self-worth and self-doubt. This can make it difficult to form relationships and lead to a lack of confidence in oneself.

- Anxiety and depression: Neglect wounds can lead to anxiety and depression as individuals struggle to manage their emotions and form healthy relationships.

- Difficulty with trust: Individuals who have experienced neglect wounds may struggle with trust, as they have not received consistent care and attention in the past. This can lead to difficulty in forming and maintaining relationships.

- Difficulty with emotional regulation: Neglect wounds can make it difficult for individuals to regulate their emotions, leading to feelings of anger, frustration, and sadness.

- Difficulty forming healthy relationships: Individuals who have experienced neglect wounds may struggle to form healthy relationships with others, as they may not have learned healthy relationship patterns growing up.

- Substance abuse: Neglect wounds can lead to substance abuse as individuals try to cope with their emotions in unhealthy ways.

- Lack of self-care: Individuals who have experienced neglect wounds may struggle with self-care, leading to neglect of their physical and emotional needs.

- Difficulty setting boundaries: Neglect wounds can make it difficult for individuals to set and maintain healthy emotional boundaries, leading to a lack of self-care and a sense of control.

The Impact of Neglect Wounds

Neglect wounds can have a profound impact on an individual's emotional and psychological well-being. Neglect is a form of childhood trauma that can have long-lasting effects on a person's sense of self, relationships, and emotional regulation. Neglect wounds can impact an individual's emotional, cognitive, and behavioral development, leading to a range of negative outcomes.

One of the most significant impacts of neglect wounds is on an individual's sense of self-worth. Neglect can lead to negative beliefs about oneself, including feelings of worthlessness, self-doubt, and insecurity. Individuals who have experienced neglect wounds may struggle with low self-esteem and a lack of confidence in themselves. This can make it difficult to form and maintain healthy relationships and can lead to a sense of social isolation.

Neglect wounds can also impact emotional regulation, making it difficult for individuals to manage their emotions in healthy ways. Neglect can lead to difficulty in identifying, expressing, and regulating emotions, resulting in heightened emotional responses and difficulty in developing emotional connections with others. This can lead to feelings of anger, frustration, and sadness, which can be difficult to cope with without healthy coping mechanisms.

In addition to emotional regulation, neglect wounds can impact an individual's ability to form healthy relationships. Neglect can lead to difficulties in developing and maintaining social connections, which can have long-lasting effects on a person's mental health and well-being.

Individuals who have experienced neglect wounds may struggle with trust and intimacy, leading to difficulty forming and maintaining healthy relationships.

Neglect wounds can also lead to unhealthy coping mechanisms, such as substance abuse or self-harm. Individuals who have experienced neglect wounds may turn to these behaviors as a way to cope with their emotions and feelings of loneliness and isolation.

Finally, neglect wounds can impact an individual's ability to set and maintain healthy emotional boundaries. This can lead to a lack of self-care and a sense of control, making it difficult for individuals to regulate their emotions and form healthy relationships.

Strategies for Addressing Neglect Wounds

Strategies for addressing neglect wounds involve adapting cognitive-behavioral therapy (CBT) and other therapeutic techniques to the specific needs of individuals who have experienced neglect. While each individual's experience with neglect is unique, there are several strategies that can be effective in addressing neglect wounds.

Adapting CBT for Neglect Wounds

Cognitive-behavioral therapy (CBT) is a widely used therapeutic technique that can be adapted to address neglect wounds. CBT involves identifying negative thought patterns and replacing them with positive ones, which can be particularly useful in addressing the negative beliefs that individuals who have experienced neglect may hold about themselves. CBT can help individuals identify and challenge negative thoughts and beliefs, leading to greater self-esteem and confidence.

CBT can also be adapted to address emotional regulation and relationship patterns. Individuals who have experienced neglect wounds may struggle with regulating their emotions and forming healthy relationships. CBT can help individuals develop healthy coping mechanisms for managing emotions and learning to form healthy relationships with others.

Other Techniques for Addressing Neglect Wounds

In addition to CBT, there are several other techniques that can be effective in addressing neglect wounds. These include:

- Mindfulness practices: Mindfulness practices, such as meditation or yoga, can help individuals develop greater awareness of their emotions and thought patterns, leading to a greater ability to regulate emotions and form healthy relationships.

- Journaling: Journaling can be a useful tool for processing emotions and gaining insight into patterns of behavior and thought. It can help individuals identify negative beliefs and patterns that may be holding them back and develop a more positive and compassionate view of themselves.

- Inner child work: Inner child work involves exploring and healing the wounds of the past through the perspective of the inner child. This can involve techniques such as visualization, guided meditation, and creative expression. Inner child work can help individuals connect with and address the root causes of their neglect wounds, leading to greater healing and growth.

Addressing neglect wounds requires a multifaceted approach that involves adapting therapeutic techniques to the specific needs of individuals who have experienced neglect. Strategies for addressing neglect wounds include adapting CBT for neglect wounds, as well as using mindfulness practices, journaling, and inner child work. It is important for individuals to seek support and guidance from mental health professionals or trusted support systems and to approach the healing journey with self-compassion and perseverance. By addressing neglect wounds, individuals can find a sense of inner peace and self-love, leading to greater emotional and psychological well-being.

Chapter 9: Addressing Abuse Wounds through Inner Child Work

Abuse is a form of childhood trauma that can have long-lasting effects on an individual's emotional and psychological well-being. Abuse can impact a person's sense of self-worth, emotional regulation, and ability to form healthy relationships and can lead to unhealthy coping mechanisms. Addressing abuse wounds is an important step toward healing and growth. By recognizing the common signs of abuse wounds and understanding their impact, individuals can begin to take steps towards healing through inner child work and other therapeutic techniques.

In this chapter, we will explore strategies for addressing abuse wounds through inner child work. We will begin by identifying common signs of abuse wounds and the impact that abuse wounds can have on an individual's emotional and psychological well-being. We will then discuss strategies for addressing abuse wounds, including adapting cognitive-behavioral therapy (CBT) for abuse wounds and other therapeutic techniques.

Addressing abuse wounds is a challenging and complex process, but it is an essential step toward healing and growth. By working through the wounds of the past, individuals can find a sense of inner peace and self-love, leading to greater emotional and psychological well-being. It is important for individuals to seek support and guidance from mental health professionals or trusted support systems and to approach the healing journey with self-compassion and perseverance.

Identifying Abuse Wounds

Identifying abuse wounds is an important step toward addressing and healing the impact of childhood trauma. Abuse is a form of childhood trauma that can take many forms, including physical, emotional, and sexual abuse. The impact of abuse wounds can be significant and long-lasting, affecting an individual's emotional and psychological well-being.

Common Signs of Abuse Wounds

The signs of abuse wounds can vary depending on the type and severity of the abuse experienced. However, there are some common signs of abuse wounds that individuals may experience, including:

- Low self-esteem: Individuals who have experienced abuse may struggle with feelings of worthlessness and self-doubt. This can impact their ability to form and maintain healthy relationships and can lead to a lack of confidence in oneself.

- Trust issues: Individuals who have experienced abuse may struggle with trust, making it difficult to form and maintain healthy relationships. This can lead to a sense of social isolation and difficulty in developing emotional connections with others.

- Emotional regulation difficulties: Abuse can impact an individual's ability to manage their emotions in healthy ways, leading to heightened emotional responses and difficulty in developing emotional connections with others.

- Negative thought patterns: Individuals who have experienced abuse may hold negative beliefs about themselves, including feelings of shame, guilt, and self-blame. This can impact their self-esteem and sense of self-worth.

- Substance abuse or self-harm: Individuals who have experienced abuse may turn to unhealthy coping mechanisms, such as substance abuse or self-harm, as a way to cope with their emotions and feelings of loneliness and isolation.

The Impact of Abuse Wounds

The impact of abuse wounds can be significant and long-lasting, affecting an individual's emotional and psychological well-being. Abuse can impact an individual's sense of self-worth, emotional regulation, and ability to form healthy relationships and can lead to unhealthy coping mechanisms.

One of the most significant impacts of abuse wounds is on an individual's sense of self-worth. Abuse can lead to negative beliefs about oneself, including feelings of shame, guilt, and self-blame. Individuals who have experienced abuse may struggle with low self-esteem and a lack of confidence in oneself, making it difficult to form and maintain healthy relationships.

Abuse wounds can also impact emotional regulation, making it difficult for individuals to manage their emotions in healthy ways. Abuse can lead to difficulty in identifying, expressing, and regulating emotions, resulting in heightened emotional responses and difficulty in developing emotional connections with others.

In addition to emotional regulation, abuse wounds can impact an individual's ability to form healthy relationships. Abuse can lead to difficulties in developing and maintaining social connections, which can have long-lasting effects on a person's mental health and well-being. Individuals who have experienced abuse wounds may struggle with trust and intimacy, leading to difficulty forming and maintaining healthy relationships.

Abuse wounds can also lead to unhealthy coping mechanisms, such as substance abuse or self-harm. Individuals who have experienced abuse may turn to these behaviors as a way to cope with their emotions and feelings of loneliness and isolation.

Strategies for Addressing Abuse Wounds

Addressing abuse wounds is an important step toward healing and growth for individuals who have experienced childhood trauma. Abuse can take many forms, including physical, emotional, and sexual abuse, and can have a long-lasting impact on an individual's emotional and psychological well-being. Strategies for addressing abuse wounds include adapting cognitive-behavioral therapy (CBT) for abuse wounds and other therapeutic techniques.

Adapting CBT for Abuse Wounds

Cognitive-behavioral therapy (CBT) is a type of therapy that is often used to address negative thought patterns and behaviors. It is a structured, short-term therapy that focuses on identifying and changing negative thought patterns and behaviors. CBT can be adapted for abuse wounds by addressing the negative beliefs and emotions associated with abuse.

One way that CBT can be adapted for abuse wounds is by focusing on identifying and challenging negative thought patterns. Individuals who have experienced abuse may hold negative beliefs about themselves, including feelings of shame, guilt, and self-blame. Through CBT, individuals can learn to identify these negative beliefs and challenge them with evidence-based thinking. This can help individuals to develop a more positive self-image and increase their self-esteem.

Another way that CBT can be adapted for abuse wounds is by addressing emotional regulation difficulties. Abuse can impact an individual's ability to manage their emotions in healthy ways, leading to heightened emotional responses and difficulty in developing emotional connections with others. Through CBT, individuals can learn techniques for regulating their emotions, such as mindfulness and relaxation techniques.

CBT can also be adapted for abuse wounds by addressing relationship difficulties. Individuals who have experienced abuse may struggle with trust and intimacy, leading to difficulty forming and maintaining healthy relationships. Through CBT, individuals can learn skills for building and maintaining healthy relationships, such as communication and boundary-setting skills.

Other Techniques for Addressing Abuse Wounds

In addition to CBT, there are other therapeutic techniques that can be effective in addressing abuse wounds.

One such technique is eye movement desensitization and reprocessing (EMDR). It is often used to treat post-traumatic stress disorder (PTSD) but can also be effective in addressing abuse wounds. It was initially developed to treat individuals who were suffering from post-traumatic stress disorder (PTSD), but it has since been used to treat a wide range of other mental health conditions as well.

During an EMDR session, the individual will be asked to recall a traumatic memory while also focusing on a specific external stimulus, such as the therapist's finger moving back and forth, a sound, or a sensation. The goal of this process is to stimulate the brain's natural healing mechanisms and allow the individual to process the traumatic memory in a safe and supportive environment.

EMDR is typically broken down into eight phases:

1. History and Treatment Planning: The therapist will gather information about the individual's history and symptoms and work with them to develop a treatment plan.
2. Preparation: The therapist will help the individual develop coping strategies and relaxation techniques to prepare them for the EMDR process.
3. Assessment: The therapist will identify the specific traumatic memories that the individual will be working on during the EMDR process.

4. Desensitization: The therapist will guide the individual through recalling the traumatic memory while focusing on the external stimulus, allowing them to process the memory in a safe and supportive environment.

5. Installation: The therapist will work with the individual to develop positive beliefs and emotions related to the traumatic memory.

6. Body Scan: The therapist will help the individual identify any residual physical sensations related to the traumatic memory and work with them to release these sensations.

7. Closure: The therapist will guide the individual through relaxation techniques and coping strategies to help them feel grounded and safe after the session.

8. Re-evaluation: The therapist will assess the individual's progress and make any necessary adjustments to the treatment plan.

Another technique is trauma-focused cognitive behavioral therapy (TF-CBT). TF-CBT, or trauma-focused cognitive behavioral therapy, is a specific type of therapy that is designed to help individuals who have experienced trauma, including abuse, to process and cope with the impact of the trauma. It is a structured therapy that includes elements of cognitive-behavioral therapy (CBT) and other techniques that are specifically geared toward addressing trauma-related symptoms.

The goal of TF-CBT is to help individuals develop coping skills to deal with the effects of the trauma, as well as to process the traumatic memories in a safe and supportive environment. The therapy is typically delivered over a period of 12-16 weeks and includes individual therapy sessions with a trained therapist.

TF-CBT is designed to be flexible and adaptable to the needs of the individual and can be used with individuals of all ages, from children to adults. The therapy is typically broken down into several stages, including:

- Psychoeducation: The first stage of TF-CBT involves educating the individual about the impact of trauma on the brain and body, as well as about the symptoms of trauma-related disorders such as post-traumatic stress disorder (PTSD).

- Skills training: The second stage of TF-CBT involves teaching the individual coping skills to deal with the symptoms of trauma, such as relaxation techniques and stress management.

- Trauma narrative: The third stage of TF-CBT involves helping the individual to process the traumatic memories by creating a narrative of the trauma. This can be done through verbal or written storytelling or through other creative means such as drawing or painting.

- Cognitive processing: The fourth stage of TF-CBT involves helping the individual to process the negative beliefs and emotions associated with the trauma and to develop more adaptive and positive beliefs and coping strategies.
- Conjoint therapy: The final stage of TF-CBT involves working with the individual and their family members or caregivers to address any issues related to the trauma within the family system.

Mindfulness-based techniques, such as meditation and breathing exercises, can also be effective in addressing abuse wounds. These techniques can help individuals to regulate their emotions and manage stress, which can be particularly helpful for those who have experienced childhood trauma.

Seeking Support

Addressing abuse wounds can be a challenging and complex process, and it is important for individuals to seek support from mental health professionals or trusted support systems. A mental health professional can help individuals to develop a personalized treatment plan that addresses their unique needs and challenges.

It is also important for individuals to approach the healing journey with self-compassion and perseverance. Healing from childhood trauma can be a difficult and emotional process, and it is important for individuals to be patient with themselves and celebrate small victories along the way.

It is important to remember that healing from abuse wounds is a process, and it may take time to see progress. However, with perseverance and self-compassion, individuals can experience meaningful growth and healing. It is never too late to begin the healing journey and prioritize one's emotional and psychological well-being.

In conclusion, addressing abuse wounds through inner child work and therapeutic techniques is a powerful step toward healing and growth. Adapting cognitive-behavioral therapy (CBT) for abuse wounds, utilizing other therapeutic techniques such as EMDR and mindfulness-based techniques, and seeking support from mental health professionals or trusted support systems are effective strategies for addressing abuse wounds. It is important to approach the healing journey with self-compassion and perseverance, as healing from childhood trauma is a process that requires time and dedication. By prioritizing one's emotional and psychological well-being, individuals can find a sense of inner peace and self-love, leading to a more fulfilling and meaningful life.

Chapter 10: Addressing Trauma through Inner Child Work

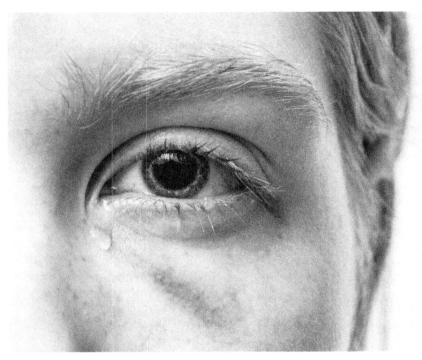

Trauma can have a profound impact on an individual's life, affecting their emotional well-being, relationships, and overall quality of life. Trauma can occur as a result of a wide range of experiences, including physical, sexual, or emotional abuse, neglect, natural disasters, accidents, or other traumatic events. Addressing trauma wounds is a critical step in the healing process, and inner child work can be an effective approach to addressing trauma-related symptoms.

Chapter 10 will focus on addressing trauma wounds through inner child work. This chapter will begin by discussing the common signs of trauma wounds and the impact that trauma can have on an individual's life. It will explore the ways in which trauma can impact an individual's emotional regulation, relationships, and overall sense of well-being.

The chapter will then delve into strategies for addressing trauma wounds, including adapting cognitive-behavioral therapy (CBT) for trauma wounds. CBT is a structured and evidence-based therapy that is widely used in the treatment of trauma-related symptoms. The chapter will discuss how CBT can be adapted to address trauma wounds, including strategies for identifying and challenging negative thought patterns and developing coping skills to deal with trauma-related symptoms.

In addition to CBT, the chapter will explore other techniques for addressing trauma wounds, including Eye Movement Desensitization and Reprocessing (EMDR), mindfulness-based therapies, and other trauma-focused therapies. The chapter will discuss the benefits of each technique and provide guidance on how to choose the best approach based on an individual's unique needs and circumstances.

Throughout the chapter, the importance of inner child work in addressing trauma wounds will be emphasized. Inner child work can be a powerful tool for healing trauma wounds by allowing individuals to access and process traumatic memories and emotions in a safe and supportive environment. The chapter will explore how inner-child work can be integrated into trauma-focused therapies and provide practical guidance on how to incorporate inner-child work into the healing process.

Overall, addressing trauma wounds through inner child work is a critical step in the healing process for individuals who have experienced trauma. This chapter will provide a comprehensive overview of the common signs and impact of trauma wounds, as well as strategies for addressing trauma wounds through CBT, EMDR, mindfulness-based therapies, and other trauma-focused therapies. By incorporating inner child work into the healing process, individuals can access a powerful tool for healing trauma wounds and moving towards emotional freedom and self-love.

Identifying Trauma Wounds

Trauma can have a profound impact on an individual's life, affecting their emotional well-being, relationships, and overall quality of life. Trauma can occur as a result of a wide range of experiences, including physical, sexual, or emotional abuse, neglect, natural disasters, accidents, or other traumatic events. Identifying trauma wounds is a critical step in the healing process, and inner child work can be an effective approach to addressing trauma-related symptoms.

Common Signs of Trauma Wounds

Trauma wounds can manifest in a variety of ways and can have a significant impact on an individual's emotional and physical health. Some common signs of trauma wounds include:

- Avoidance: Individuals who have experienced trauma may avoid situations or activities that remind them of the traumatic event. This can include avoiding certain people, places, or situations and can lead to social isolation and difficulty in functioning in everyday life.

- Intrusive thoughts or memories: Trauma can lead to intrusive thoughts or memories of the traumatic event, which can be distressing and can interfere with an individual's ability to concentrate or focus on other tasks.

- Hyperarousal: Trauma can also lead to hyperarousal, which can manifest in a variety of ways. This can include difficulty sleeping, constantly feeling on edge or irritable, and an exaggerated startle response.

- Negative beliefs or feelings: Trauma can lead to negative beliefs or feelings about oneself or the world around them. Individuals who have experienced trauma may struggle with feelings of guilt or shame or may feel a sense of hopelessness or despair.

- Emotional dysregulation: Trauma can also lead to emotional dysregulation, which can manifest in a variety of ways. This can include difficulty managing emotions, difficulty with impulse control, and a tendency to engage in self-destructive behaviors.

Understanding the Impact of Trauma Wounds

Trauma wounds can have a profound impact on an individual's life, affecting their emotional well-being, relationships, and overall quality of life. Some common ways in which trauma can impact an individual's life include:

- Emotional regulation: Trauma can make it difficult for individuals to regulate their emotions, leading to mood swings, emotional dysregulation, and difficulty with impulse control.

- Relationships: Trauma can also impact an individual's relationships, making it difficult to trust others or form close connections with others. Individuals who have experienced trauma may struggle with intimacy or may have difficulty maintaining healthy relationships.

- Physical health: Trauma can also impact an individual's physical health, leading to a variety of symptoms, such as headaches, gastrointestinal problems, and chronic pain.

- Self-esteem: Trauma can also impact an individual's self-esteem and sense of self-worth, leading to feelings of shame, guilt, or a sense of worthlessness.

Overall, identifying trauma wounds is a critical step in the healing process for individuals who have experienced trauma. By understanding the common signs and impacts of trauma wounds, individuals can begin to seek out the help and support that they need to begin the healing process.

Inner child work can be a powerful tool for healing trauma wounds by allowing individuals to access and process traumatic memories and emotions in a safe and supportive environment.

Strategies for Addressing Trauma Wounds

Adapting CBT for Trauma Wounds

Adapting cognitive-behavioral therapy (CBT) for trauma wounds involves tailoring the approach to the specific needs of individuals who have experienced trauma. Trauma can have a profound impact on the way people think, feel, and behave, and adapting CBT to address these effects requires a sensitive and nuanced approach.

CBT is a therapeutic approach that focuses on the relationship between thoughts, feelings, and behaviors. It is based on the idea that negative thoughts and beliefs can lead to negative emotions and behaviors and that by changing these negative thought patterns, individuals can improve their emotional well-being and change negative behaviors. CBT is often used to treat a wide range of mental health conditions, including anxiety disorders, depression, and post-traumatic stress disorder (PTSD).

When adapting CBT for trauma wounds, therapists may use a range of techniques that specifically address the unique challenges associated with trauma. These techniques may include gradual exposure, cognitive restructuring, and behavioral activation.

Gradual exposure involves exposing individuals to the source of their trauma in a safe and supportive environment in a way that is gradual and controlled. This can help individuals develop new associations with the traumatic memory or trigger and reduce the emotional intensity of their response. This technique may be particularly helpful for individuals with PTSD, who may experience intense feelings of fear or anxiety when exposed to triggers associated with their trauma.

Cognitive restructuring involves helping individuals identify and challenge negative thought patterns and beliefs related to the trauma. For example, individuals may hold beliefs such as "I am responsible for what happened to me" or "I am not safe in the world." By identifying and challenging these negative beliefs, individuals can develop more adaptive and positive ways of thinking about their trauma.

Behavioral activation involves encouraging individuals to engage in positive, rewarding activities that they may have lost interest in due to their trauma. This can help individuals develop a sense of mastery and accomplishment, which can counteract feelings of helplessness or hopelessness associated with trauma.

It is important to note that while CBT can be effective for treating trauma wounds, it is not a one-size-fits-all approach. Adapting CBT to address trauma wounds requires a sensitivity to the unique needs and experiences of each individual. Therapists who work with trauma survivors need to be trained in trauma-informed care and have experience working with this population.

In addition to CBT, other therapeutic approaches may also be effective in treating trauma wounds, such as Eye Movement Desensitization and Reprocessing (EMDR) and Trauma-Focused CBT (TF-CBT). These approaches may be particularly helpful for individuals with more severe trauma symptoms or for individuals who have experienced multiple traumas.

Other techniques for Addressing Trauma Wounds (such as EMDR or TF-CBT)

In addition to cognitive-behavioral therapy (CBT), there are other techniques that can be used to address trauma wounds, such as Eye Movement Desensitization and Reprocessing (EMDR) and Trauma-Focused CBT (TF-CBT). These approaches are particularly effective for individuals who have experienced severe trauma or have multiple trauma wounds.

EMDR is a therapeutic approach that involves bilateral stimulation, which can take the form of eye movements, auditory tones, or physical tapping. This technique helps to reprocess traumatic memories and reduce the emotional distress associated with them. EMDR involves eight phases of treatment, including history taking, preparation, desensitization, installation, body scan, closure, reevaluation, and maintenance. During the desensitization phase, the individual is asked to recall the traumatic memory while simultaneously focusing on the bilateral stimulation. This process helps to reduce the emotional intensity of the traumatic memory and promotes a more adaptive response.

TF-CBT is a specialized form of CBT that is specifically designed to address trauma wounds in children and adolescents. This approach involves eight to 20 sessions of treatment and focuses on helping children and adolescents process their traumatic experiences, develop coping skills, and build a support system. TF-CBT involves several key components, including psychoeducation, relaxation techniques, affective modulation, cognitive processing, and parent-child sessions. This approach is often used to treat PTSD, anxiety, depression, and other mental health conditions that may result from childhood trauma.

In addition to these specific techniques, there are also several other strategies that can be helpful in addressing trauma wounds. These include:

- Mindfulness: Mindfulness involves paying attention to the present moment without judgment. This approach can help individuals develop a greater awareness of their thoughts and emotions and develop greater emotional regulation skills.

- Creative arts therapy: Creative arts therapy involves the use of art, music, or other creative outlets to help individuals express their emotions and process their trauma wounds. This approach can be particularly helpful for individuals who have difficulty verbalizing their experiences.

- Group therapy: Group therapy involves participating in therapy sessions with other individuals who have experienced similar trauma wounds. This approach can help individuals develop a sense of community and support and gain perspective on their experiences.

Overall, there are several techniques and approaches that can be effective in addressing trauma wounds. The key is to work with a trained therapist who can tailor treatment to the individual's unique needs and experiences. With the right support and treatment, individuals can recover from trauma wounds and improve their emotional well-being.

Inner Child Work as A Strategy for Addressing Trauma Wounds

Inner child work is a therapeutic approach that involves exploring and healing the wounded inner child, which is the part of us that carries the unresolved pain and trauma from our childhood. The goal of inner child work is to help individuals connect with their inner child, identify and heal the wounds, and promote emotional healing and growth.

Inner child work can be a powerful strategy for addressing trauma wounds because it helps individuals access the root cause of their pain and develop greater self-awareness and self-compassion. By acknowledging and validating the inner child's experiences, individuals can learn to release negative patterns of thinking and behavior that have been holding them back and develop more adaptive coping strategies.

There are several key principles of inner child work, including:

- Developing a safe and nurturing environment: Inner child work requires a safe and supportive environment that allows individuals to explore their innermost thoughts and emotions without fear of judgment or criticism. This can be achieved through the therapeutic relationship, as well as through practices such as mindfulness and self-care.

- Connecting with the inner child: In order to heal the inner child, individuals must first learn to connect with this wounded aspect of themselves. This can involve visualization exercises, journaling, or other techniques that help individuals access their innermost thoughts and feelings.

- Validating the inner child's experiences: Inner child work involves validating the inner child's experiences and acknowledging the impact of childhood trauma on adult life. This process can be difficult and painful, but it is essential for healing and growth.

- Developing self-compassion: Inner child work emphasizes the importance of self-compassion, which involves treating oneself with kindness, understanding, and acceptance. By developing greater self-compassion, individuals can learn to release negative patterns of self-talk and develop greater self-esteem and self-worth.

- Inner child work can be incorporated into a variety of therapeutic approaches, including CBT, psychodynamic therapy, and mindfulness-based therapies. Some common techniques used in inner child work include:

- Visualization exercises: Visualization exercises involve imagining the wounded inner child and connecting with their emotions and experiences. This can be a powerful tool for developing empathy and understanding of the inner child.

- Journaling: Journaling involves writing down one's thoughts and feelings in a safe and supportive environment. This can help individuals process their emotions and gain greater self-awareness.

- Inner child dialogues: Inner child dialogues involve having a conversation with the wounded inner child and helping them process their emotions and experiences. This can be a powerful tool for promoting healing and growth.

- Reparenting exercises: Reparenting exercises involve developing a nurturing and supportive relationship with oneself, which can help to heal the wounded inner child and promote emotional healing.

Overall, inner child work can be a powerful strategy for addressing trauma wounds and promoting emotional healing and growth. By developing greater self-awareness, self-compassion, and empathy for the wounded inner child, individuals can learn to release negative patterns of thinking and behavior and develop more adaptive coping strategies.

Creating A Safe and Supportive Environment for Inner Child Work

Creating a safe and supportive environment is crucial for inner child work to be effective in addressing trauma wounds. The inner child may feel vulnerable and afraid to express emotions or memories related to past trauma, and it's important to establish a safe space where they feel comfortable to do so.

Some strategies for creating a safe and supportive environment for inner child work include:

- Establishing trust: Trust is essential in any therapeutic relationship, but it's especially important when working with the inner child. The therapist must build trust with the client to create a safe space for them to share their experiences and emotions. This can be achieved by being empathetic, non-judgmental, and validating the client's experiences.

- Encouraging self-compassion: The inner child may hold feelings of shame and guilt related to past trauma, and it's important to encourage self-compassion. The therapist can help the client develop a compassionate inner voice to counteract negative self-talk.

- Providing a sense of control: Trauma can leave individuals feeling powerless and out of control. The therapist can help the client regain a sense of control by allowing them to make decisions about their therapy and progress.

- Practicing grounding techniques: Grounding techniques can help the inner child feel safe in the present moment. These techniques can include deep breathing, visualization, and mindfulness exercises.

- Addressing any safety concerns: It's important to address any safety concerns related to the client's trauma history. This can include discussing safety plans and developing coping strategies for triggering situations.

By creating a safe and supportive environment, inner child work can help individuals address trauma wounds and move towards healing and growth.

Building Resilience as A Key Aspect of Inner Child Work

Building resilience is a key aspect of inner child work as it helps individuals develop the skills and resources needed to cope with future stressors and challenges. Resilience is the ability to adapt and bounce back from difficult experiences, and it can be developed through intentional practices. Some strategies for building resilience as part of inner child work include:

- Identifying and addressing negative thought patterns: Negative self-talk can hinder resilience and keep individuals stuck in a cycle of self-doubt and shame. Through inner child work, individuals can identify negative thought patterns and learn to challenge them with more positive and realistic self-talk.

- Developing a growth mindset: A growth mindset is the belief that skills and abilities can be developed through hard work and effort. Inner child work can help individuals develop a growth mindset by identifying strengths and setting achievable goals for personal growth.

- Practicing self-care: Self-care is essential for building resilience as it helps individuals manage stress and maintain overall well-being. Inner child work can help individuals identify self-care practices that work for them and incorporate them into their daily routines.

- Developing healthy coping strategies: Coping strategies are tools individuals use to manage stress and difficult emotions. Inner child work can help individuals identify healthy coping strategies that work for them, such as mindfulness, exercise, or creative expression.

- Building a support network: A strong support network is an essential part of resilience-building. Inner child work can help individuals identify sources of support, such as friends, family, or support groups, and develop healthy communication and boundaries within these relationships.

By building resilience, individuals can better navigate the challenges of life and bounce back from adversity. Inner child work can provide a foundation for developing resilience by identifying strengths and building a sense of self-efficacy and self-worth.

Exploring Inner Child Wounds

Exploring inner child wounds related to trauma is a crucial aspect of healing and recovery. By identifying these wounds, individuals can gain a deeper understanding of how they impact their present-day life and begin the process of healing.

Some common inner child wounds related to trauma include:

- Abandonment: Feeling abandoned or neglected by a caregiver can lead to a sense of insecurity and mistrust in relationships.

- Betrayal: Betrayal by a trusted individual can lead to difficulty trusting others and a fear of vulnerability.

- Rejection: Rejection or exclusion from a social group or peer can lead to feelings of worthlessness and low self-esteem.

- Shame: Experiencing shame can lead to a negative self-image and a fear of being judged by others.

- Guilt: Feelings of guilt can lead to self-blame and self-criticism and make it difficult to forgive oneself.

The impact of these wounds on present-day life can be profound, affecting relationships, self-esteem, emotional regulation, and more. For example, someone who experienced abandonment as a child may struggle with trusting others and forming close relationships. Someone who experienced rejection may struggle with low self-esteem and social anxiety. Someone who experienced betrayal may struggle with vulnerability and opening up to others.

Exploring these wounds through inner child work involves a deep dive into the past to identify specific events or experiences that led to the wound. It also involves understanding how these wounds have manifested in the present-day and how they impact behavior, thoughts, and emotions.

Through inner child work, individuals can begin to heal these wounds by developing self-compassion, challenging negative beliefs, and building resilience. By exploring and healing inner child wounds related to trauma, individuals can experience greater emotional freedom, self-awareness, and self-love.

Addressing Trauma in Children

Addressing trauma in children requires unique considerations and strategies to adapt trauma work for their developmental stage and level of understanding. The support of parents and caregivers is also critical in helping children heal their inner child wounds.

Some unique considerations for addressing trauma wounds in children include:

- Age-appropriate language and techniques: Trauma work for children must be adapted to their developmental stage and level of understanding. This may involve using age-appropriate language and techniques, such as art therapy or play therapy, to help children express their emotions.

- Creating a safe and supportive environment: It is essential to create a safe and supportive environment for trauma work with children. This may involve building a trusting relationship with the child, providing a quiet and comfortable space, and using calming techniques such as deep breathing or mindfulness.

- Involving parents and caregivers: Parents and caregivers play a crucial role in supporting their child's inner child healing. They can provide emotional support, encourage the child to express their emotions and participate in therapy sessions with their child.

Strategies for adapting trauma work for children may include:

- Creative expression: Children may find it challenging to express their emotions verbally. Creative expression through art, play, or storytelling can help children process their emotions in a non-threatening way.

- Positive coping skills: Teaching children positive coping skills, such as deep breathing, mindfulness, or physical activity, can help them regulate their emotions and cope with stress.

- Family therapy: Family therapy can be an effective way to involve parents and caregivers in the healing process and improve family communication and relationships.

The role of parents and caregivers in supporting children's inner child healing cannot be overstated. By providing emotional support, encouraging the expression of emotions, and participating in therapy sessions, parents and caregivers can help children feel safe and supported in the healing process.

In summary, addressing trauma in children requires unique considerations and strategies to adapt trauma work for their developmental stage and level of understanding. Creating a safe and supportive environment, involving parents and caregivers, and using age-appropriate language and techniques are essential in helping children heal their inner child wounds. By adapting trauma work for children and providing the necessary support, children can experience greater emotional freedom, self-awareness, and resilience.

Chapter 11: The Role of Positive Affirmations in Inner Child Healing

Embarking on the journey of inner child healing can be an incredibly transformative experience filled with self-discovery, growth, and a deepening connection to oneself. As you navigate this path, it's essential to equip yourself with tools that foster self-compassion, resilience, and positivity. One such powerful tool is the practice of positive affirmations. By harnessing the potential of these empowering statements, you can create lasting, positive change in your life and the way you relate to your inner child.

In this chapter, we will delve into the remarkable world of positive affirmations, exploring their impact on inner child healing and the science behind their effectiveness. You will learn practical strategies for creating and using affirmations tailored to address specific inner child wounds and discover how to seamlessly incorporate them into your daily life. We will also discuss the challenges you might encounter as you integrate affirmations into your healing journey and provide insights to overcome them.

Furthermore, we will examine the intimate connection between positive affirmations, self-compassion, and self-care, highlighting how these practices can support your emotional well-being and self-esteem. You'll also find a collection of sample affirmations that can be customized to suit your unique needs and guide you in your quest for personal growth.

Embrace the transformative power of positive affirmations as you continue on your path to healing your inner child. By nurturing a mindset of self-love and empowerment, you will create a solid foundation for lasting change, emotional stability, and overall well-being. So let's embark on this journey together and unlock the incredible potential of positive affirmations for inner child healing.

The Power of Positive Affirmations

The Impact of Positive Affirmations on Inner Child Healing

Positive affirmations are powerful tools that can greatly impact the process of inner child healing. By using these simple yet potent statements, you have the ability to reshape the way you think about yourself, your past, and your future. Healing the inner child requires addressing the emotional wounds and negative beliefs you have carried with you since childhood, and positive affirmations can play a crucial role in this transformative journey.

As you work on healing your inner child, positive affirmations can help you shift your focus away from painful memories and towards a more loving and compassionate relationship with yourself. This can create a supportive environment for healing, enabling you to cultivate self-acceptance, forgiveness, and empathy for the child within you. As you consistently practice positive affirmations, you'll notice improvements in your self-esteem, confidence, and emotional resilience, which can further accelerate the healing process.

How Positive Affirmations Work

Positive affirmations work by gradually replacing the negative thought patterns and limiting beliefs that have taken root in your mind over time. These empowering statements help you consciously direct your thoughts towards more constructive and uplifting ideas, encouraging a shift in your mindset and emotional state. When you repeatedly expose yourself to positive affirmations, you're essentially "rewiring" your brain to focus on the positive aspects of your life, which can ultimately lead to a more optimistic outlook and greater self-compassion.

The Science Behind Positive Affirmations

The efficacy of positive affirmations is backed by scientific research, which has shown that these uplifting statements can lead to significant psychological and physiological changes. Studies have found that positive affirmations can activate areas of the brain associated with self-processing and self-reward, leading to increased self-esteem, self-compassion, and overall well-being.

One of the key principles underlying the effectiveness of positive affirmations is the concept of neuroplasticity. This refers to the brain's ability to adapt and change in response to new experiences and stimuli. By consistently practicing positive affirmations, you are effective "training" your brain to form new neural connections that support these affirmative thoughts, ultimately fostering a more positive mindset.

Reprogramming Negative Beliefs Through Positive Affirmations

One of the most important aspects of inner child healing is addressing and transforming the negative beliefs that have taken root during childhood. These limiting beliefs can have a profound impact on your self-perception, self-worth, and overall mental health. By incorporating positive affirmations into your healing journey, you can work towards reprogramming these negative beliefs and replacing them with more empowering and compassionate thoughts.

To effectively reprogram your negative beliefs, it's essential to create affirmations that directly counteract these thoughts. For example, if you struggle with feelings of unworthiness, you might create affirmations such as "I am deserving of love and happiness" or "I am worthy of success and abundance." By consistently repeating these affirmations, you'll reinforce the belief that you are, indeed, deserving and worthy, which can help to shift your mindset and emotional state.

It's important to be patient with yourself as you work on reprogramming your negative beliefs, as this process can take time and persistence. Remember, the limiting beliefs you're working to transform have been ingrained in your mind for many years, and it will likely take consistent practice and dedication to fully replace them with more positive and affirming thoughts. By remaining committed to this practice, however, you'll likely experience profound shifts in your self-perception, emotional well-being, and overall healing journey.

Using Positive Affirmations in Inner Child Healing

Strategies For Creating and Using Positive Affirmations

Tailoring Affirmations to Address Specific Inner Child Wounds

When using positive affirmations for inner child healing, it's essential to tailor your affirmations to address the specific wounds and emotional issues that you are working on. By doing this, you can create a powerful tool that directly targets the areas where you need the most healing and support.

To create tailored affirmations, begin by identifying the specific wounds or limiting beliefs that you are trying to heal. This might include feelings of abandonment, unworthiness, guilt, or shame, for example. Once you have identified the areas that need healing, you can then craft affirmations that directly counteract these negative beliefs and emotions. For instance, if you struggle with feelings of abandonment, you might create affirmations like "I am lovable and worthy of connection" or "I am surrounded by love and support."

Visualization and affirmations for enhanced healing

Combining visualization with positive affirmations can significantly enhance the healing process. By creating vivid mental images that complement your affirmations, you engage multiple senses and deepen the emotional impact of the experience. This can help to further anchor the positive messages in your subconscious mind, reinforcing your new beliefs and promoting lasting change.

To incorporate visualization into your affirmation practice, close your eyes and imagine a scene that represents the feeling or outcome you want to achieve through the affirmation. For example, if your affirmation is "I am deserving of love and happiness," you might visualize yourself surrounded by loving friends and family, feeling joyful and content. As you recite your affirmation, hold this image in your mind and allow yourself to fully experience the emotions associated with it.

Combining affirmations with other healing modalities

Positive affirmations can be even more powerful when combined with other healing modalities, such as meditation, journaling, therapy, or energy healing. By integrating affirmations into these practices, you create a multi-faceted approach to inner child healing that addresses the emotional, mental, and energetic aspects of your healing journey.

For example, you might recite positive affirmations during meditation practice, focusing your attention on the words and the feelings they evoke. Alternatively, you could incorporate affirmations into your journaling routine by writing them down and reflecting on the emotions and insights they bring up. By combining affirmations with other healing modalities, you can create a holistic and comprehensive approach to inner child healing that facilitates profound transformation and growth.

How To Incorporate Positive Affirmations into Daily Life

Establishing a daily affirmation routine

Integrating positive affirmations into your daily life is crucial for creating lasting change and supporting your inner child's healing journey. By establishing a consistent routine, you can reinforce your new beliefs and gradually reprogram your subconscious mind to embrace a more positive, compassionate, and nurturing mindset.

To create a daily affirmation routine, choose a specific time each day to recite your affirmations. This could be first thing in the morning, during a break at work, or before going to bed at night. Find a quiet space where you can focus and be present with your affirmations, and take a few moments to connect with your breath and center yourself. As you recite your affirmations, speak them aloud with conviction, and allow yourself to fully feel the emotions they evoke.

Using affirmations in moments of emotional distress

In addition to your daily affirmation practice, it's essential to use affirmations in moments of emotional distress or when you're struggling with negative thoughts and emotions. By doing this, you can interrupt the cycle of negative thinking and replace it with more supportive and empowering beliefs.

When you notice yourself becoming emotionally distressed or caught up in negative thoughts, take a moment to pause and acknowledge what's happening. Then, choose a relevant affirmation to counteract the negative emotions and repeat it to yourself, either silently or aloud. For example, if you're feeling unworthy or unlovable, you might recite an affirmation like "I am deserving of love and kindness" or "I am enough just as I am." As you repeat the affirmation, focus on the positive emotions it evokes and allow them to replace the negative feelings you were experiencing.

Creating an affirmation journal or vision board

Another effective way to incorporate positive affirmations into your daily life is by creating an affirmation journal or vision board. An affirmation journal is a dedicated space where you can write down your affirmations, along with any reflections, insights, or experiences related to your inner child healing journey. Regularly writing and reviewing your affirmations can help you to internalize the positive messages and maintain your focus on the healing process.

A vision board is a visual representation of your affirmations, goals, and aspirations. To create a vision board, collect images, quotes, and other visual elements that represent the feelings and outcomes you want to achieve through your inner child healing work. Arrange these elements on a poster or corkboard, and place your vision board in a prominent location where you can see it daily. By regularly viewing your vision board, you can remind yourself of your affirmations and maintain a positive, healing-focused mindset.

Utilizing technology to support affirmation practice

In today's technology-driven world, there are numerous tools and resources available to help you incorporate positive affirmations into your daily life. Smartphone apps, for example, can be a convenient way to access and practice your affirmations, allowing you to receive reminders or notifications throughout the day. Some apps even offer guided affirmation sessions, helping you to focus and deepen your practice.

Additionally, you can use digital voice recorders or smartphone recording features to record yourself reciting your affirmations. Listening to these recordings can be a powerful way to reinforce the positive messages, as you hear your own voice expressing the affirmations with conviction and emotion. You can also find numerous affirmation videos, podcasts, or guided meditations online, providing further support for your inner child healing journey.

In conclusion, using positive affirmations as part of your inner child healing process can have a profound impact on your emotional well-being and overall personal growth. By creating tailored affirmations, incorporating visualization, and integrating affirmations with other healing modalities, you can effectively address your inner child's wounds and promote lasting change. Establishing a daily affirmation routine, utilizing technology, and creating visual reminders of your affirmations can further support your healing journey, helping you to cultivate a more compassionate, nurturing, and empowered mindset.

Overcoming Challenges with Positive Affirmations

While positive affirmations can be a powerful tool in your inner child healing journey, some people may encounter challenges or skepticism when trying to incorporate them into their lives. In this section, we will discuss ways to address skepticism and resistance, debunk common misconceptions about positive affirmations, and provide tips for making affirmations more effective and believable.

Addressing Skepticism and Resistance to Using Affirmations

- Understanding the root cause of skepticism and resistance: It is crucial to identify the underlying reasons for your skepticism or resistance to positive affirmations. Some common reasons may include past experiences with failed self-help techniques, a belief that affirmations are too simplistic, or a general lack of trust in the process. Once you understand the root cause, you can begin to address it and open yourself up to the benefits of positive affirmations.

- Educate yourself on the science behind affirmations: A great way to address skepticism is to learn about the science behind affirmations and their impact on the brain. Numerous studies have shown that positive affirmations can influence our thoughts, emotions, and behavior by activating the brain's reward and self-regulation systems. Understanding the science behind affirmations can help you see them as a valid and effective tool for inner child healing.

- Start small and build up: If you're skeptical or resistant to using affirmations, begin with small, easy-to-believe statements and gradually work your way up to more complex and challenging affirmations. This approach can help you build trust in the process and experience the benefits firsthand.

Common Misconceptions About Positive Affirmations

- Positive affirmations are just wishful thinking: Many people believe that affirmations are merely statements of wishful thinking that do not have any real impact on their lives. However, research has shown that affirmations can change our thought patterns, emotions, and behavior. By repeating positive affirmations, we can rewire our brains and create new neural pathways that support healthier and more positive beliefs.

- Positive affirmations are a quick fix: Some people may view affirmations as a magical solution that will instantly solve all their problems. While affirmations can be a powerful tool in your inner child healing process, it is essential to remember that they are just one part of a more extensive healing journey. Incorporating affirmations into your daily routine can support and enhance the work you do in therapy or through other healing modalities, but they are not a standalone solution.

- You must always feel positive for affirmations to work: Another misconception is that you must feel positive and happy for affirmations to be effective. However, the purpose of affirmations is not to suppress negative emotions but rather to help you create healthier thought patterns and beliefs. It is entirely normal to have doubts or feel negative emotions while using affirmations, but with practice and consistency, you can gradually shift your mindset.

Tips for Making Affirmations More Effective and Believable

- Personalize your affirmations: Ensure that your affirmations are specific and relevant to your inner child healing process. Tailor your affirmations to address your unique experiences, emotions, and beliefs. Personalized affirmations will be more meaningful and have a more significant impact on your healing journey.

- Use present tense and positive language: When crafting your affirmations, use present tense and positive language to create a sense of immediacy and empowerment. Instead of saying, "I will be confident," say, "I am confident." This approach helps your brain accept the affirmation as a current reality rather than a distant goal.

- Emphasize feeling and emotion: Connect with the emotions and feelings behind your affirmations. When you say an affirmation, try to feel the emotions associated with it, such as confidence, love, or safety.

- Practice regularly and consistently: Consistency is key to the effectiveness of affirmations. Set aside time each day to practice your affirmations, either by speaking them aloud, writing them down, or visualizing them. The more you repeat your affirmations, the stronger the neural pathways in your brain will become, making it easier to adopt new, positive beliefs.

- Combine affirmations with other healing techniques: To maximize the benefits of positive affirmations, combine them with other healing modalities such as therapy, journaling, meditation, or mindfulness practices. This holistic approach can help reinforce the positive beliefs and thought patterns you are cultivating through your affirmations.

- Be patient and persistent: Changing deeply ingrained beliefs and thought patterns takes time and effort. It is essential to remain patient and persistent in your affirmation practice, even if you do not see immediate results. Over time, you will begin to notice subtle shifts in your thoughts, emotions, and behavior as your affirmations take effect.

- Address any negative self-talk or beliefs: As you practice your affirmations, you may notice negative thoughts or beliefs that arise in response to your positive statements. Rather than ignoring or suppressing these negative thoughts, acknowledge them and explore their origins. This process can help you identify and challenge the underlying beliefs that are holding you back in your inner child healing journey.

- Seek support and accountability: Share your affirmation practice with a trusted friend, family member, or therapist who can provide support, encouragement, and accountability. Having someone else to share your journey with can make it easier to stay consistent in your practice and maintain motivation.

Positive Affirmations and Self-Care

The Connection Between Positive Affirmations and Self-Compassion

Positive affirmations and self-compassion are closely linked, as both are powerful tools for personal growth, healing, and self-improvement. Self-compassion is the practice of treating ourselves with the same kindness, understanding, and empathy we would offer to a loved one in times of struggle or pain.

Positive affirmations can help foster self-compassion by reinforcing the idea that we deserve love, care, and understanding. By regularly practicing positive affirmations, we can cultivate a more nurturing and supportive inner dialogue, replacing self-criticism and judgment with kindness and acceptance. This shift in our internal narrative allows us to be more resilient in the face of adversity and to maintain a sense of self-worth and emotional balance.

Developing a Self-Care Routine That Incorporates Affirmations

A self-care routine that incorporates positive affirmations can help support your inner child's healing process and promote overall well-being. Here are some strategies to create a self-care routine that includes affirmations:

- Establish a morning and evening routine: Begin and end each day with a series of positive affirmations tailored to your specific needs and goals. This practice can help set the tone for your day and provide a sense of closure and reflection at night.

- Incorporate mindfulness practices: Combine your affirmations with mindfulness techniques such as deep breathing exercises, meditation, or yoga. These practices can help you stay present and focused on your affirmations, enhancing their effectiveness.

- Use affirmations during self-care activities: Incorporate affirmations into your regular self-care activities, such as exercise, journaling, or creative expression. For example, repeat your affirmations while running, walking, or engaging in other physical activities. This can help reinforce the positive beliefs you are cultivating through your affirmation practice.

- Create a self-care space: Designate a special area in your home or workspace for practicing affirmations and self-care. This space should be free of distractions and dedicated to relaxation and reflection. Surround yourself with items that inspire you, such as calming music, scented candles, or inspiring artwork.

Using Affirmations to Enhance Self-Esteem and Self-Worth

Positive affirmations can be a powerful tool for enhancing self-esteem and self-worth, as they helped to reframe negative beliefs and thought patterns that may be holding you back from fully embracing your true self. Here are some ways to use affirmations to improve your self-esteem and self-worth:

- Reflect on the aspects of your self-esteem and self-worth that could use some strengthening. Consider any negative beliefs or thought patterns you may be holding onto and create affirmations that directly challenge these beliefs.

- Develop affirmations that resonate with your unique experiences and goals. These affirmations should be specific, positive, and focused on your desired outcomes. For example, if you struggle with self-confidence, an affirmation such as "I am capable and strong" can be a powerful reminder of your inherent abilities.

- As you recite your affirmations, visualize yourself embodying the positive qualities you are affirming. Imagine yourself experiencing success, happiness, and fulfillment as a result of your newfound self-esteem and self-worth. This visualization can help to reinforce the positive beliefs you are cultivating through your affirmation practice.

- Consistency is crucial when it comes to using affirmations to enhance self-esteem and self-worth. Commit to practicing your affirmations regularly, ideally every day, to ensure that your new, positive beliefs become deeply ingrained in your subconscious mind.

- Reach out to friends, family, or a therapist to share your experiences and progress with affirmations. They can offer encouragement and guidance and help keep you accountable on your journey toward improved self-esteem and self-worth.

- While affirmations are a powerful tool for shaping your mindset, it's important to also take concrete steps to improve your self-esteem and self-worth. Set realistic goals, challenge yourself, and engage in activities that build your confidence and sense of accomplishment.

- Remember that cultivating self-esteem and self-worth takes time and effort. Be patient with yourself as you work through the process, and practice self-compassion when you encounter setbacks or challenges.

- As you progress in your journey towards greater self-esteem and self-worth, your affirmations may need to evolve to reflect your new beliefs and goals. Regularly review your affirmations and revise them as needed to ensure they continue to support your personal growth and development.

- Recognize that you deserve love, kindness, and understanding, and strive to treat yourself with the same compassion you would offer to a loved one. By embracing self-compassion, you create a nurturing environment for your affirmations to take root and flourish, ultimately leading to a stronger sense of self-esteem and self-worth.

Examples of Positive Affirmations for Inner Child Healing

As you embark on your inner child healing journey, using positive affirmations can be an incredibly powerful tool. These affirmations can be tailored to address various inner child wounds, personalized to suit your individual needs, and applied to specific areas of life such as relationships and careers. In this section, we will explore sample affirmations for different inner child wounds and provide tips for personalizing them to support your healing process.

Sample Affirmations Addressing Various Inner Child Wounds

Abandonment:

- "I am worthy of love and belonging."
- "I am never alone because I am always surrounded by love and support."
- "I am safe and secure in my relationships."

Emotional neglect:

- "My feelings are valid and important."
- "I am allowed to express my emotions openly and honestly."
- "I have the right to be heard and understood."

Physical or emotional abuse:

- "I am strong and resilient."
- "I deserve to be treated with kindness and respect."
- "I am no longer defined by my past experiences."

Enmeshment or codependency:

- "I am allowed to have my own thoughts and feelings."
- "I am separate from others and can make decisions for myself."
- "It is healthy for me to set boundaries and assert my needs."

Invalidation:

- "My thoughts and feelings are valid and important."
- "I am allowed to be my true, authentic self."
- "I trust my intuition and inner wisdom."

Tips for personalizing affirmations to suit individual needs:

- Reflect on your personal experiences: Spend some time reflecting on your childhood experiences and the inner child wounds you want to heal. This will help you create affirmations that are specific to your unique needs and experiences.

- Use your own words: Write your affirmations using language that feels natural and authentic to you. Avoid using words or phrases that feel forced or insincere, as this can make it harder for you to connect with the affirmation.

- Be specific: When crafting your affirmations, try to be as specific as possible about the beliefs or patterns you want to change. For example, instead of simply saying, "I am confident," try saying, "I am confident in my ability to speak up for myself and set boundaries."

- Use present tense: Frame your affirmations in the present tense, as if the desired belief or feeling is already true. This helps to shift your mindset from one of lack or deficiency to one of abundance and empowerment.

Creating Affirmations for Specific Areas of Life

Relationships:

- "I am worthy of love and respect from others."

- "I am capable of maintaining healthy and fulfilling relationships."

- "I am open to giving and receiving love in all forms."

Career:

- "I am skilled and competent in my chosen profession."

- "I deserve success and abundance in my career."

- "I am capable of achieving my career goals and aspirations."

Personal growth:

- "I am constantly evolving and growing into the best version of myself."

- "I am open to learning and embracing new experiences."

- "I have the courage and determination to overcome any challenges I face."

Health and well-being:

- "I am committed to taking care of my physical and emotional health."

- "I deserve to feel good in my body and mind."

- "I am in control of my well-being and make choices that support my health."

By incorporating these tips and examples into your affirmation practice, you can create powerful, personalized affirmations that address your unique inner child wounds and support your healing journey. Remember that consistency is key when it comes to using affirmations effectively.

Incorporate them into your daily routine and repeat them regularly to reinforce the new beliefs and thought patterns you are working to establish.

It's important to be patient with yourself as you work with affirmations. Healing and transformation take time, and it may take a while before you start to notice significant changes in your mindset and emotional state. However, with persistence and dedication, you can gradually shift your thought patterns and create a more positive, empowered outlook on life.

As you progress in your inner child healing journey, don't be afraid to revisit and revise your affirmations. As you grow and change, your needs and priorities may evolve, and it's essential to adapt your affirmations to reflect your current situation and goals. By continually updating and refining your affirmation practice, you can ensure that it remains a powerful and relevant tool for supporting your healing process.

Long-Term Benefits of Positive Affirmations in Inner Child Healing

As you embark on your journey of inner child healing, incorporating positive affirmations can have a significant and lasting impact on your overall personal growth and well-being. In this section, we will explore the long-term benefits of consistent affirmation practice, including how it can lead to greater emotional stability, resilience, and a more fulfilling life.

The Lasting Impact of Consistent Affirmation Practice

Consistency is a crucial aspect of any personal growth or healing practice, and it is especially true when it comes to working with positive affirmations. The more consistently you practice affirmations, and the more profound and lasting their effects will be on your thoughts, emotions, and behavior. As you integrate affirmations into your daily life, you begin to change the neural pathways in your brain, gradually replacing old, limiting beliefs with new, empowering ones.

Over time, these new thought patterns become more deeply ingrained, leading to lasting shifts in your mindset, emotional state, and overall outlook on life. By consistently practicing affirmations, you can create a strong foundation for long-term healing and personal growth, enabling you to overcome obstacles and challenges more easily and to live a more fulfilling and authentic life.

How Affirmations Can Lead to Overall Personal Growth and Well-Being

Positive affirmations can have far-reaching effects on various aspects of your life, contributing to overall personal growth and well-being. As you work to heal your inner child and reprogram negative beliefs, you may notice improvements in several areas of your life, including:

1. As you develop a more positive and empowered mindset through affirmations, you may find that your relationships with others improve as well. When you cultivate self-compassion, self-worth, and self-esteem, you are more likely to attract and maintain healthy, supportive relationships with others.

2. With increased self-confidence and a more optimistic outlook on life, you may find it easier to pursue your career goals and achieve professional success. Affirmations can help you to cultivate a growth mindset, enabling you to view challenges and setbacks as opportunities for learning and growth rather than barriers to success.

3. Your mental and emotional well-being can have a significant impact on your physical health. By working with affirmations to cultivate a more positive mindset, you may experience improvements in your physical health, such as increased energy, better sleep, and a stronger immune system.

4. As you reprogram your thoughts and beliefs through affirmations, you may find that your mental health improves as well. Affirmations can help to reduce symptoms of anxiety, depression, and other mental health challenges, enabling you to experience greater emotional stability and overall well-being.

Strengthening Resilience and Emotional Stability Through Affirmations

One of the most significant long-term benefits of incorporating positive affirmations into your inner child healing journey is the development of greater resilience and emotional stability. Resilience refers to your ability to bounce back from adversity and cope effectively with stress and challenges.

By consistently practicing affirmations, you can strengthen your emotional resilience in several ways:

- Affirmations can help you to focus on your strengths, accomplishments, and potential for growth rather than dwelling on your shortcomings and past hurts. This shift in perspective can enable you to approach challenges with a more optimistic and solution-oriented mindset.

- As you use affirmations to develop greater self-compassion and self-worth, you become more adept at managing your emotions and coping with stress. You learn to treat yourself with kindness and understanding rather than being overly critical or harsh when faced with setbacks or difficulties.

- Regularly working with affirmations can also help you to become more aware of your emotions and to develop healthier ways of managing them. By acknowledging and validating your feelings, you can learn to respond to emotional triggers in a more balanced and constructive manner rather than being overwhelmed or controlled by them.

- Through consistent affirmation practice, you can foster a more robust sense of self, which can serve as a foundation for emotional stability. By gaining a deeper understanding of your values, strengths, and aspirations, you become better equipped to navigate life's challenges with resilience and confidence.

- Positive affirmations can encourage you to seek out and cultivate supportive relationships, both with yourself and others. Building a strong network of friends, family, and professional support can be an essential component of emotional resilience, as it provides you with a safety net to lean on during difficult times.

Chapter 12: Cultivating Self-Love through Inner Child Healing

Welcome to Chapter 12: Cultivating Self-Love through Inner Child Healing. In this transformative chapter, we will dive deep into the heart of self-love, a vital component in the journey of healing your inner child. As you embark on this powerful journey, you will unlock the ability to nurture and cherish your innermost self, paving the way to a happier, more fulfilled life.

Self-love is a concept that is often misunderstood or undervalued in today's fast-paced world. However, it is an essential aspect of personal growth and a crucial factor in the healing of our inner child. In this chapter, we will clarify the true meaning of self-love, cutting through the misconceptions and revealing its vital role in the inner child healing process. You will discover that self-love is not about indulgence, vanity, or selfishness but rather a profound and empowering form of self-acceptance and self-care.

Understanding the importance of self-love in inner child healing requires exploring the deep connection between our childhood experiences and our present self-perception. As we journey through life, the wounds of our past often shape the way we view ourselves, resulting in limiting beliefs and negative self-talk. By cultivating self-love, we can break free from these detrimental patterns, allowing our inner child to heal and flourish.

In the subsequent sections, we will delve into the practical strategies for cultivating self-love. These methods will guide you in developing a strong and lasting connection with your inner self, empowering you to embrace your true worth and potential. As you learn to treat yourself with the kindness, compassion, and understanding that you deserve, you will notice a profound transformation in your emotional well-being and overall quality of life.

This chapter is an invitation to embark on a journey of self-discovery, self-compassion, and self-empowerment. As you learn to nurture and care for your inner child, you will find that the love you give to yourself reverberates throughout every aspect of your life. Relationships will strengthen, career opportunities will blossom, and a sense of peace and contentment will take root within your soul.

By cultivating self-love through inner child healing, you are giving yourself the ultimate gift: the permission to be your authentic self, free from the shackles of past wounds and limiting beliefs. Embrace this journey with an open heart and an open mind, and witness the incredible transformation that unfolds within you.

So, are you ready to explore the depths of self-love and unlock the powerful healing potential within? Let's begin this life-changing journey together, step by step, and uncover the boundless love that lies within your heart. Remember, you deserve love, happiness, and fulfillment, and the path to achieving these starts with embracing and nurturing your inner child.

Understanding Self-Love

Defining Self-Love

Self-love is a multifaceted concept that encompasses a variety of elements, including self-acceptance, self-compassion, self-care, and self-respect. At its core, self-love is the practice of acknowledging and embracing our inherent worth and value, despite our perceived flaws, mistakes, or shortcomings. It is the ability to treat ourselves with kindness, understanding, and patience, just as we would with a dear friend or loved one.

The term self-love may seem simple, but it carries a profound significance in our lives. True self-love involves recognizing that we are worthy of love, care, and happiness, regardless of our past experiences or external circumstances. It means honoring our unique journey and embracing the totality of who we are, including our strengths, vulnerabilities, and imperfections.

To cultivate self-love, we must first cultivate self-awareness. By becoming more in tune with our thoughts, emotions, and behaviors, we can identify the areas in which we may be neglecting or undermining our own well-being. This heightened awareness allows us to make conscious choices and take deliberate actions that support our growth, healing, and overall happiness.

Understanding The Importance of Self-Love in Inner Child Healing

The connection between self-love and inner child healing is both profound and essential. Our inner child represents the emotional and psychological aspects of our early years, which continue to influence our thoughts, feelings, and behaviors in adulthood. The wounds and traumas we experience during childhood often result in negative self-beliefs and patterns of self-sabotage, which can hinder our ability to experience self-love and maintain healthy relationships.

In the context of inner child healing, self-love plays a crucial role in addressing these wounds and fostering emotional resilience. By cultivating self-love, we create a safe and nurturing environment in which our inner child can heal, grow, and thrive. This process enables us to release the limiting beliefs and emotional baggage that have been holding us back, allowing us to step into our power and embrace our true potential.

The importance of self-love in inner child healing cannot be overstated. When we approach our healing journey from a place of self-compassion and self-acceptance, we create a solid foundation upon which lasting transformation can occur. In doing so, we not only heal our inner child but also pave the way for greater happiness, fulfillment, and overall well-being.

The benefits of self-love in inner child healing are numerous and far-reaching, including:

- Enhanced self-esteem: As we learn to love and accept ourselves unconditionally, our self-esteem and self-worth naturally increase. This newfound confidence enables us to pursue our goals, dreams, and passions with greater determination and persistence.

- Improved mental and emotional health: Cultivating self-love promotes a healthier relationship with our thoughts and emotions, allowing us to better manage stress, anxiety, and depression. As a result, we experience greater peace, balance, and emotional stability.

- Healthier relationships: By practicing self-love, we set the stage for healthier, more fulfilling relationships with others. When we value and respect ourselves, we are better equipped to establish and maintain boundaries, communicate effectively, and form deep connections with those around us.

- Greater resilience: When we nurture our inner child with love and compassion, we develop the emotional resilience needed to navigate life's challenges and setbacks. This inner strength empowers us to bounce back from adversity and continue moving forward on our healing journey.

Strategies for Cultivating Self-Love

- Self-compassion is the act of treating ourselves with the same kindness, understanding, and empathy that we would extend to a loved one. To cultivate self-compassion, acknowledge your emotions and feelings without judgment, and remind yourself that everyone experiences pain and struggles. Instead of harshly criticizing yourself, offer words of encouragement and support.

- Setting boundaries is crucial for maintaining a healthy relationship with ourselves and others. Establishing and maintaining clear boundaries demonstrates self-respect and helps protect our emotional and mental well-being. Take time to identify your limits and communicate them assertively with others to ensure a balanced and harmonious life.

- Self-care encompasses a wide range of activities and practices aimed at promoting physical, emotional, and mental well-being. Prioritize self-care by incorporating regular exercises, a balanced diet, adequate sleep, and stress-reducing activities, such as meditation or yoga, into your daily routine. Additionally, engage in hobbies and interests that bring joy and fulfillment to your life.

- Developing self-awareness is crucial for fostering self-love. By becoming more in tune with your thoughts, emotions, and behaviors, you can identify areas of improvement and make necessary adjustments. Practice mindfulness and introspection through journaling, meditation, or therapy to gain insight into your internal world.

- Invest time and energy in personal development to build self-love. Pursue new skills, knowledge, or experiences that enrich your life and contribute to your sense of purpose. By actively working on your growth, you demonstrate self-love and reinforce the belief that you are worthy of happiness and success.

- The people and environments we surround ourselves with have a significant impact on our self-perception and emotional well-being. Seek out relationships and social circles that uplift, support, and inspire you. Distance yourself from toxic or unhealthy influences that may hinder your ability to cultivate self-love.

- Holding onto past hurts and resentments can prevent us from embracing self-love. Practice forgiveness by acknowledging your pain and releasing any grudges or negative emotions you may be harboring. Forgiving yourself for past mistakes and perceived shortcomings is also essential for fostering self-love and self-compassion.

- Recognizing and celebrating your achievements, both big and small, is an important aspect of self-love. Acknowledge your successes and give yourself credit for your hard work and dedication. By celebrating your accomplishments, you reinforce your self-worth and build confidence in your abilities.

- Negative self-talk can be a significant barrier to cultivating self-love. Learn to identify and challenge these destructive thought patterns by questioning their validity and replacing them with more constructive and supportive beliefs. This process takes time and practice but is essential for fostering a healthy self-image.

- Cultivating an attitude of gratitude can have a profound impact on your ability to love and appreciate yourself. By regularly acknowledging the positive aspects of your life, you shift your focus away from perceived flaws and shortcomings. Keep a gratitude journal, or take a few moments each day to mentally list the things you are grateful for.

- A visualization is a powerful tool for personal growth and self-love. Spend time each day visualizing your ideal self – the person you aspire to be. This practice can help you clarify your goals, values, and desires and inspire you to take action toward becoming your best self.

- Positive affirmations are statements that reinforce and promote self-love, self-worth, and self-acceptance. Repeat affirmations daily, such as "I am worthy of love and happiness" or "I am enough, just as I am." By consistently practicing positive affirmations, you can gradually reprogram your subconscious beliefs and cultivate a more loving and compassionate relationship with yourself.

- Recognize that nobody is perfect, and imperfections are a natural part of the human experience. Embrace your unique qualities, flaws, and quirks, and appreciate them for making you who you are. By accepting and loving yourself unconditionally, you create a foundation for self-love and inner healing.

- If you find it challenging to cultivate self-love on your own, consider seeking the guidance of a mental health professional, such as a therapist or counselor. They can help you explore the underlying issues contributing to your lack of self-love and provide tools and strategies to promote healing and personal growth.

- Cultivating self-love is a lifelong journey, and it's essential to be patient with yourself as you navigate this path. Remember that progress may be slow and nonlinear, and setbacks are a natural part of the process. Be kind and gentle with yourself as you work towards building a more loving and compassionate relationship with yourself.

In conclusion, self-love is a critical component of inner child healing and overall well-being. By implementing these strategies, you can cultivate a deep and lasting sense of self-love that supports your healing journey and empowers you to live a more authentic, fulfilling, and joyful life. Remember that self-love is an ongoing practice, and it takes time, effort, and dedication to nurture and maintain. Be patient with yourself as you embark on this transformative journey, and trust that the rewards of self-love will be well worth the effort.

Maintaining a Self-Love Journal

The journey to cultivate self-love is an ongoing process that requires introspection, self-awareness, and continuous self-improvement. One powerful tool that can help foster self-love is maintaining a self-love journal. In this section, we will explore the benefits of journaling for self-love, how to start and maintain a self-love journal, and how to incorporate gratitude, self-reflection, and self-affirmation in your journaling practice.

The Benefits of Journaling for Self-Love

- Enhances self-awareness: Writing in a self-love journal can help you become more self-aware by providing a safe space to explore and express your thoughts, emotions, and experiences. By recording your feelings and experiences, you can gain insights into your patterns, habits, and beliefs, allowing you to make necessary changes for personal growth.

- Encourages self-expression: Journaling is a form of self-expression that can help you give voice to your inner thoughts and feelings. By putting your emotions and experiences into words, you can better understand and process them, which can lead to a greater sense of self-acceptance and self-love.

- Promotes self-care: A self-love journal can serve as a reminder to prioritize self-care and make time for activities that nourish and support your well-being. By recording your self-care activities and their effects on your mood and energy levels, you can identify the practices that are most beneficial for you.

- Foster's emotional resilience: Journaling can help you develop emotional resilience by allowing you to process and release difficult emotions in a healthy way. Writing about your challenges, setbacks, and frustrations can help you gain perspective, learn from your experiences, and cultivate a more positive and resilient mindset.

How to Start and Maintain a Self-Love Journal

1. Choose a journal: Select a journal that resonates with you, whether it be a simple notebook, a fancy leather-bound journal, or a digital app. The most important thing is to choose a format that you enjoy and feel comfortable using.

2. Set aside time: Dedicate a specific time each day or week to write in your self-love journal. This could be in the morning when you wake up, before bed, or during a break in your day. Consistency is key to developing a regular journaling practice.

3. Create a comfortable environment: Find a quiet, comfortable space where you can write without distractions. This could be a cozy corner of your home, a favorite coffee shop, or a peaceful outdoor setting.

4. Use prompts: If you're unsure what to write about, consider using journal prompts to guide your self-love practice. Prompts can help you explore different aspects of self-love, such as self-compassion, self-forgiveness, and self-acceptance.

Incorporating Gratitude, Self-Reflection, and Self-Affirmation in Your Journaling Practice

1. Gratitude: Focusing on gratitude is a powerful way to shift your mindset and cultivate self-love. In your self-love journal, make a daily or weekly list of things you're grateful for. This practice can help you recognize the positive aspects of your life and foster a greater sense of appreciation and contentment.

2. Self-reflection: Use your journal to reflect on your thoughts, emotions, and behaviors. By examining your experiences and reactions, you can identify patterns and beliefs that may be hindering your self-love journey. Self-reflection can also help you set intentions and goals for personal growth and self-improvement.

3. Self-affirmation: Incorporate positive affirmations into your journaling practice to reinforce self-love and self-acceptance. Write down affirmations that resonate with you and reflect the qualities and strengths you wish to cultivate. Some examples of self-affirmations include:

   - "I am worthy of love and respect."

   - "I am capable of overcoming challenges and achieving my goals."

   - "I accept myself for who I am, and I am proud of my accomplishments."

   Revisit your affirmations regularly and recite them aloud or silently to yourself. This practice can help you replace negative self-talk with more empowering and supportive thoughts.

4. Celebrate achievements: Use your self-love journal to record and celebrate your achievements, both big and small. By acknowledging your successes, you reinforce the belief in your abilities and build self-confidence.

5. Track your progress: Keep track of your personal growth and self-improvement by documenting your self-love journey in your journal. Reflect on your entries to recognize the progress you've made and identify areas where you may need additional focus and effort.

6. Practice self-compassion: Remember to be kind and gentle with yourself as you engage in your self-love journaling practice. Treat yourself with the same compassion, understanding, and encouragement that you would offer to a close friend or loved one.

Maintaining a self-love journal can be a transformative tool in your journey toward greater self-love and self-acceptance. By incorporating gratitude, self-reflection, and self-affirmation into your journaling practice, you can foster a deeper connection with yourself, cultivate emotional resilience, and create a more positive and loving relationship with yourself. Embrace this practice as a valuable component of your inner child healing process and witness the positive impact it can have on your overall well-being and personal growth.

Building Healthy Boundaries for Self-Love

Developing self-love is an essential component of inner child healing and overall emotional well-being. One critical aspect of self-love that often goes overlooked is the establishment of healthy boundaries. Personal boundaries are the limits and rules we set for ourselves within relationships, dictating how we expect to be treated and how we will treat others in return. By setting and maintaining healthy boundaries, we can protect our emotional, mental, and physical well-being while also fostering deeper, more fulfilling relationships with others. In this section, we will discuss the relationship between self-love and personal boundaries and provide techniques for establishing and maintaining healthy boundaries in your life.

Understanding the Relationship between Self-Love and Personal Boundaries

Self-love involves recognizing and valuing our own needs, desires, and well-being. It means treating ourselves with kindness, compassion, and respect, regardless of external circumstances or the opinions of others. Establishing healthy boundaries is an essential aspect of self-love because it communicates to ourselves and others that our feelings, thoughts, and needs are important and worthy of respect.

When we have weak or nonexistent boundaries, we are more likely to tolerate unhealthy behavior from others, neglect our own needs, and allow others to take advantage of us. This can lead to feelings of resentment, burnout, and low self-esteem. By establishing and maintaining healthy boundaries, we can protect our emotional and mental health, foster a sense of self-worth, and create more balanced, fulfilling relationships with those around us.

Techniques for Establishing and Maintaining Healthy Boundaries

- Develop self-awareness: The first step in establishing healthy boundaries is to develop a clear understanding of your own needs, values, and limits. Spend time reflecting on your experiences, feelings, and beliefs to determine what types of boundaries are most important to you.

- Communicate clearly: Once you have identified your boundaries, communicate them clearly and assertively to others. This may involve expressing your feelings, stating your needs, or setting limits on specific behaviors. Remember that it is not selfish to prioritize your well-being and assert your needs – it is a necessary part of self-care and self-love.

- Be consistent: Consistency is key when it comes to maintaining healthy boundaries. Be prepared to reinforce your boundaries when they are challenged or crossed, even if doing so feels uncomfortable at first. This may involve repeating your requests, standing your ground, or even ending relationships that consistently disrespect your boundaries.

- Respect the boundaries of others: Just as you have the right to establish and maintain your own boundaries, it is essential to respect the boundaries of others. This may involve listening to their needs, empathizing with their feelings, and accepting their limits without judgment or resentment.

- Practice self-compassion: Establishing healthy boundaries can be challenging, especially if you have a history of prioritizing the needs of others over your own. Be gentle with yourself as you navigate this process, and remember that setting boundaries is an act of self-love and self-care.

Asserting Your Needs and Respecting the Needs of Others

When we assert our needs and respect the needs of others, we create an environment of mutual understanding, trust, and respect. This can lead to more balanced and fulfilling relationships, both with ourselves and with others. Here are some tips for asserting your needs while respecting the needs of others:

- When expressing your needs, use "I" statements to describe your feelings and desires rather than placing blame or making accusations. For example, instead of saying, "You always ignore me," say, "I feel ignored when you don't respond to my messages."

- When others express their needs or boundaries, listen actively and empathetically. Validate their feelings and acknowledge their perspective, even if you don't necessarily agree with it. This can help create a sense of understanding and trust between you and the other person.

- In some situations, finding a middle ground between your needs and the needs of others may be necessary. Be open to compromise and look for solutions that can accommodate both parties' needs while still respecting your own boundaries.

- Establishing and maintaining healthy boundaries is a process that takes time and practice. Be patient with yourself and others as you work towards cultivating self-love and mutual respect in your relationships.

- If you find it challenging to establish and maintain healthy boundaries, consider seeking support from a therapist, counselor, or support group. They can offer guidance, encouragement, and strategies to help you navigate this process and foster self-love and healthy relationships.

Self-Love and Physical Health

The journey of cultivating self-love is multifaceted, encompassing not only our emotional and mental well-being but also our physical health. When we prioritize self-love, we recognize the importance of nurturing our bodies and taking care of our physical needs. In this section, we will explore the connection between self-love and physical health, discuss strategies for developing healthy habits and self-care routines, and delve into the role of exercise, nutrition, and sleep in promoting self-love.

The Connection Between Self-Love and Taking Care of Your Physical Well-Being

Our physical health is intricately linked to our emotional and mental well-being. When we practice self-love, we understand that taking care of our bodies is an essential component of overall wellness. Conversely, neglecting our physical health can lead to negative emotional states and decreased self-worth.

By prioritizing our physical well-being, we send a message to ourselves that we deserve love, care, and attention. This can create a positive feedback loop in which taking care of our bodies enhances our self-esteem while a heightened sense of self-worth further motivates us to maintain healthy habits.

Strategies for Developing Healthy Habits and Self-Care Routines

Creating a self-care routine that incorporates healthy habits is vital for promoting self-love and overall well-being. Here are some strategies to help you develop a personalized self-care routine:

1. Take a close look at your current lifestyle and identify areas where improvements can be made. This could include incorporating more physical activity, adopting a healthier diet, or making time for relaxation and stress relief.

2. Establish achievable goals related to your physical health, such as committing to a weekly exercise routine or aiming to consume more fruits and vegetables each day. Make sure your goals are realistic and attainable to avoid feelings of failure or disappointment.

3. Create a daily schedule that incorporates healthy habits, such as exercise, nutritious meals, and sufficient sleep. Establishing a consistent routine can help make these activities feel like a natural part of your day, making it easier to maintain them in the long term.

4. Keep track of your progress by maintaining a journal or using a tracking app. Monitoring your achievements can help you stay motivated and provide valuable insight into areas where you may need additional support or encouragement.

5. Remember that developing healthy habits takes time and effort. Be patient with yourself and practice self-compassion if you encounter setbacks or challenges along the way.

The Role of Exercise, Nutrition, and Sleep in Promoting Self-Love

Exercise, nutrition, and sleep are three key components of physical health that play a crucial role in cultivating self-love. By prioritizing these aspects of our well-being, we can build a strong foundation for overall wellness and enhance our sense of self-worth.

1. Exercise: Engaging in regular physical activity has numerous benefits, including improved cardiovascular health, increased strength and flexibility, reduced stress, and enhanced mood. Exercise also encourages the release of endorphins, which can contribute to feelings of happiness and self-confidence. By prioritizing exercise as part of your self-care routine, you demonstrate a commitment to your well-being and reinforce your sense of self-love.

2. Nutrition: A well-balanced diet that incorporates a variety of nutrient-dense foods is essential for maintaining optimal physical health. Consuming a diet rich in fruits, vegetables, whole grains, lean proteins, and healthy fats can provide the necessary nutrients to support energy levels, immune function, and overall well-being. By choosing to nourish your body with wholesome foods, you are actively investing in your health and practicing self-love.

3. Sleep: Adequate sleep is crucial for physical and mental health. A lack of sleep can lead to a host of negative consequences, including decreased cognitive function, weakened immune system, and mood disturbance. By prioritizing quality sleep as part of your self-care routine, you give your body and mind the rest they need to function optimally. This can help you feel more energized, focused, and emotionally balanced, which can contribute to a greater sense of self-love.

Incorporating these aspects of physical health into your self-care routine can have a significant impact on your overall well-being and sense of self-love. By taking care of your body and mind in this way, you send a message to yourself that you are worthy of love and care, which can help foster a more positive self-image and enhance your ability to heal and grow from inner child wounds.

Chapter 13: Healing Your Inner Child with Art Therapy

When it comes to healing our inner child wounds, traditional talk therapy may not always be enough. Art therapy, a form of psychotherapy that utilizes the creative process to explore emotions and promote healing, can be an effective tool for addressing childhood trauma and abandonment wounds.

Art therapy encourages individuals to express themselves through various art forms, such as drawing, painting, sculpting, and collage-making. By engaging in the creative process, individuals can access and work through emotions that may be difficult to articulate verbally. Art therapy can also be a useful tool for processing traumatic memories in a safe and supportive environment.

In this chapter, we will explore the concept of art therapy and how it can be used in inner child healing. We will discuss the benefits of art therapy, strategies for incorporating it into your inner child work, and examples of art therapy exercises for healing inner child wounds. Additionally, we will explore the role of creativity in inner child healing and how it can enhance the healing journey.

It's important to note that you do not need to be an artist to benefit from art therapy. Art therapy is about the process of creating, not the final product. Anyone can engage in art therapy regardless of skill level or artistic ability.

If you are struggling to heal from childhood wounds and traditional talk therapy has not been effective, consider incorporating art therapy into your healing journey. By embracing your creativity and exploring your emotions through art, you may be able to access a deeper level of healing and promote inner-child integration.

Understanding Art Therapy

Art therapy is a form of psychotherapy that uses art-making as a means of communication, self-expression, and healing. It involves the use of various art materials, such as paint, clay, or collage, to create artwork that reflects an individual's emotions, thoughts, and experiences. The therapist works with the individual to help them explore their artwork and to gain insight and understanding about their inner world.

What is Art Therapy?

Art therapy is a form of expressive therapy that can help individuals to process and express their emotions, thoughts, and experiences in a safe and supportive environment. It can be used to address a wide range of emotional and psychological issues, including depression, anxiety, trauma, and addiction.

Art therapy is based on the belief that the creative process can be therapeutic and healing in and of itself. Through the act of creating, individuals can access parts of themselves that may be difficult to express verbally and can tap into their innate capacity for self-expression, problem-solving, and insight.

Art therapy can be practiced in a variety of settings, including hospitals, clinics, schools, and community centers. It is often used in conjunction with other forms of therapy, such as talk therapy or cognitive-behavioral therapy.

Benefits of Art Therapy for Inner Child Healing

Art therapy can be particularly beneficial for healing inner child wounds, as it allows individuals to access and express deep-seated emotions and experiences in a non-verbal way. Some of the benefits of art therapy for inner child healing include:

- Expression: Art therapy provides a safe and non-threatening way to express emotions and experiences that may be difficult to put into words.

- Empowerment: Through the act of creating, individuals can feel a sense of control and empowerment over their experiences and emotions.

- Insight: Art therapy can help individuals gain insight and understanding about their inner world and can promote self-awareness and self-reflection.

- Emotional Regulation: Art therapy can help individuals regulate their emotions by providing a means of externalizing and processing difficult emotions.

- Connection: Art therapy can promote connection and socialization, as individuals can share their artwork with others and engage in a collaborative creative process.

- Self-Esteem: Through the act of creating, individuals can develop a sense of accomplishment and self-esteem, which can help to counteract feelings of shame or inadequacy.

Overall, art therapy can be a powerful tool for promoting emotional healing and personal growth. It can be particularly effective for individuals who struggle to express themselves verbally and for those who have experienced trauma or emotional pain in childhood.

Using Art Therapy in Inner Child Healing

Inner child healing is the process of addressing and healing the emotional wounds that we have experienced in our childhood. These wounds may have resulted from various forms of trauma, neglect, or abuse and can manifest as low self-esteem, anxiety, depression, and other emotional and psychological issues. Art therapy is an effective approach to inner child healing because it allows individuals to express and explore their emotions and experiences in a safe and supportive environment. In this section, we will discuss the strategies for using art therapy in inner child work, as well as some art therapy exercises for healing inner child wounds.

Strategies for Using Art Therapy in Inner Child Work

- Create a Safe Space: Before beginning any art therapy exercise, it is important to create a safe and comfortable space. This can be achieved by setting up a private and quiet space where the you can feel secure and at ease. The you should also establish clear boundaries and expectations for the session to feel safe and supported.

- Use Art as a Tool for Expression: Art therapy is a non-verbal form of therapy, which makes it an ideal tool for exploring and expressing emotions that may be difficult to put into words. You should encourage to use art materials such as paints, crayons, and markers to express their feelings and experiences.

- Encourage Exploration and Experimentation: In inner child work, it is important for the client to explore and experiment with different art materials and techniques. This can help you to discover new ways of expressing yourselves and your emotions and can also help them to develop a sense of curiosity and creativity.

- Foster a Non-Judgmental Environment: It is important for the therapist to create a non-judgmental environment where the client can feel free to express themselves without fear of criticism or rejection. The therapist should refrain from making any value judgments about the client's artwork and should instead focus on exploring the emotions and experiences that are being expressed. If you are your own therapist do the same for yourself.

- Provide Support and Validation: The therapist should provide emotional support and validation to the client throughout the art therapy session. This can be achieved by actively listening to the client, providing empathy and understanding, and acknowledging the client's feelings and experiences.

Art Therapy Exercises for Healing Inner Child Wounds

1. Inner Child Drawing: This exercise involves asking the client to draw a picture of themselves as a child. The therapist can then ask the client to describe the picture and the emotions that they feel as they look at it. This exercise can help the client to connect with their inner child and to explore their feelings and experiences from that time in their life.

2. Guided Imagery: This exercise involves guiding the client through a visualization exercise that allows them to connect with their inner child. The therapist can ask the client to close their eyes and imagine themselves as a child and then guide them through a visualization of a safe and nurturing environment where they can connect with their inner child.

3. Collage: This exercise involves asking the client to create a collage using images and words that represent their inner child. The therapist can then ask the client to describe the collage and the emotions that they feel as they look at it. This exercise can help the client to explore their inner child and to express their emotions and experiences through visual art.

4. Puppet Play: This exercise involves using puppets to explore and express the client's emotions and experiences. The therapist can ask the client to choose a puppet that

represents their inner child and then use the puppet to act out different scenarios or emotions. This exercise can help the client to connect with their inner child in a playful and creative way.

5. Body Mapping: This exercise involves asking the client to trace their body onto a piece of paper and then use art materials to express their emotions and experiences in different parts of their body. The therapist can ask the client to use different colors and textures to represent different emotions or experiences and to talk about their artwork as they create it. This exercise can help the client to explore how their emotions and experiences are stored in their body and release any physical or emotional tension that they may be holding onto.

6. Sand Tray Therapy: This exercise involves asking the client to create a scene using miniature objects in a sand tray. The therapist can then ask the client to describe the scene and the emotions that they feel as they look at it. This exercise can help the client to explore their inner world and to express their emotions and experiences in a three-dimensional way.

7. Scribble Drawing: This exercise involves asking the client to make a random scribble on a piece of paper and then use art materials to turn the scribble into a picture. The therapist can encourage the client to be spontaneous and creative in their approach and to explore the emotions and experiences that emerge through the process. This exercise can help the client to access their inner creativity and to express their emotions in a playful and imaginative way.

8. Letter Writing: This exercise involves asking the client to write a letter to their inner child, either from their adult self or from their inner child. The therapist can encourage the client to express their feelings and experiences in the letter and to offer words of support and validation to their inner child. This exercise can help the client to develop a sense of compassion and self-acceptance and to heal any emotional wounds that they may be carrying from their childhood.

Note: If you are your own therapist then you should do the same as written above.

In summary, art therapy is a powerful tool for inner child healing, as it allows individuals to express and explore their emotions and experiences in a safe and supportive environment. By using art as a tool for expression, therapists can help clients to access their inner world and to heal emotional wounds that may have resulted from childhood trauma, neglect, or abuse. Through a variety of art therapy exercises, clients can explore and express their inner child in a creative and imaginative way and develop a greater sense of self-compassion and acceptance. As with any form of therapy, it is important for the therapist to create a safe and supportive environment and to provide emotional validation and support throughout the process.

The Role of Creativity in Inner Child Healing

Inner child healing is the process of addressing and healing the emotional wounds that we have experienced in our childhood. These wounds may have resulted from various forms of trauma, neglect, or abuse and can manifest as low self-esteem, anxiety, depression, and other emotional and psychological issues. Creativity can play an essential role in the inner child healing process by providing a safe and supportive space for exploring and expressing difficult emotions. In this section, we will discuss how creativity can help with inner child healing and provide strategies for incorporating creativity into your healing journey.

How Creativity Can Help with Inner Child Healing

- Provides a Non-Verbal Means of Expression: Sometimes, the emotions associated with inner child wounds can be difficult to express verbally. Creativity can provide a non-verbal means of expressing these emotions. Through various forms of art, such as painting, drawing, music, dance, and writing, you can access and explore emotions that you may have been suppressing for years.

- Offers a Safe and Supportive Space: Engaging in creative activities can provide a sense of freedom and playfulness, creating a relaxed and non-judgmental environment. This can allow for a sense of release and expression, providing a sense of comfort and ease as you navigate your healing journey.

- Fosters Self-Discovery and Self-Awareness: Creativity can be a powerful tool for self-discovery and self-awareness. By exploring different forms of creative expression, you can gain a better understanding of yourself and your inner world. This can help you to identify and process emotions and experiences that may have been buried deep within you.

- Provides a Sense of Control: Engaging in creative activities can provide a sense of control over your healing journey. By creating something, you are actively taking steps toward your healing and can feel a sense of accomplishment and pride.

Strategies for Incorporating Creativity into Your Healing Journey

- Find an Activity that Resonates with You: Creativity can manifest in many forms, such as painting, drawing, music, dance, writing, and more. It is important to find an activity that resonates with you. For example, if you love to dance, try exploring different forms of dance, such as contemporary, ballet, or hip-hop. If you prefer writing, try journaling or writing poetry. It is essential to find an activity that sparks your creativity and that you enjoy.

- Set Aside Time for Creative Expression: Incorporating creativity into your healing journey requires dedicated time and effort. Set aside time each day or week to engage in your chosen creative activity. It is important to prioritize this time for yourself and your healing.

- Allow Yourself to Explore and Experiment: Creativity is a process of exploration and experimentation. Allow yourself to explore different techniques, materials, and methods. The aim is not to create a masterpiece but to allow yourself to express yourself freely.

- Allow Yourself to Feel: Creativity can offer a safe space for expressing difficult emotions. Allow yourself to feel the emotions that arise during your creative expression. It is okay to feel vulnerable and exposed during this process.

- Reflect and Process: After engaging in your creative activity, take the time to reflect on your experience. How did it make you feel? What emotions did it bring up for you? What did you learn about yourself? Processing these reflections can help to deepen the healing process.

In conclusion, creativity can play an essential role in the inner child healing process. It allows for a non-verbal means of expression, a safe and supportive environment, self-discovery and self-awareness, and a sense of control over the healing journey. By finding an activity that resonates with you, setting aside time for creative expression, allowing yourself to explore and experiment, feeling your emotions, and processing your reflections, you can unlock the power of creativity to heal your inner child. Remember, your journey of inner child healing is unique, and there is no right or wrong way to incorporate creativity. Find what works for you and enjoy the journey.

Overcoming Resistance to Art Therapy in Inner Child Work

Inner child work is a therapeutic process that involves addressing and healing emotional wounds that were formed during childhood. Art therapy can be a powerful tool for this process, as it allows individuals to express and explore their emotions and experiences in a non-verbal way. However, some individuals may experience resistance toward art therapy, which can hinder their progress toward healing. We will explore common resistance to art therapy and provide strategies for overcoming resistance and embracing art therapy in inner child healing.

Common Resistance to Art Therapy

- Fear of Judgment: One of the most common forms of resistance to art therapy is fear of judgment. This fear can arise from a belief that their artwork will be judged by others or that it will reveal something negative about themselves. As a result, individuals may feel hesitant to express themselves fully or may avoid art therapy altogether.

- Self-Doubt: Self-doubt can also be a form of resistance to art therapy. Individuals may doubt their artistic abilities or worry that their artwork will not be good enough. This can lead to feelings of insecurity and may prevent individuals from engaging in the creative process.

- Trauma Triggers: Engaging in art therapy can also trigger traumatic memories and emotions for some individuals. This can be overwhelming and may lead to resistance towards art therapy.

- Limited Experience with Art: Another form of resistance can come from a lack of experience with art. If individuals have not engaged in artistic activities before, they may feel unsure of how to use art to express themselves.

Strategies for Overcoming Resistance and Embracing Art Therapy in Inner Child Healing

- Acknowledge Your Resistance: The first step in overcoming resistance is to acknowledge and accept it. It is normal to feel resistance toward something new or unfamiliar, especially when it involves addressing past trauma. By acknowledging your resistance, you can begin to understand the root causes and work towards finding ways to overcome them.

- Practice Mindfulness: Mindfulness practices can help individuals become more aware of their thoughts and feelings. This can help individuals to identify and understand their resistance to art therapy. Mindfulness practices can include deep breathing, meditation, or simply taking a few minutes each day to focus on the present moment.

- Start Small: If individuals feel overwhelmed by the idea of engaging in art therapy, they can start small. They can begin by doing simple art exercises or doodling in a journal. This can help them to become more comfortable with the creative process and build their confidence.

- Build a Support System: Building a support system can be helpful in overcoming resistance towards art therapy. This can include working with a qualified therapist who specializes in art therapy or joining a support group. Having a supportive and understanding environment can help individuals to feel more comfortable expressing themselves through art.

- Reframe Negative Beliefs: Negative beliefs about art therapy can be a significant barrier to healing. Individuals may believe that they are not creative or that art therapy will not be helpful for them. These negative beliefs can be reframed by focusing on the positive aspects of art therapy and recognizing that the creative process is not about producing a masterpiece but rather about expressing oneself.

- Use Art as a Tool for Self-Expression: Art therapy is not about producing a perfect work of art but rather about using art as a tool for self-expression. Individuals can use art to express their emotions and experiences in a way that is unique to them. They do not need to be skilled artists to benefit from art therapy.

- Be Gentle with Yourself: Healing from past trauma is a journey, and it is important to be gentle with oneself along the way. Individuals should be patient with themselves as they work through their resistance to art therapy. It is also important to recognize that healing is not a linear process, and there may be setbacks along the way. However, with time and patience, individuals can overcome their resistance to art therapy and begin to reap the benefits of this powerful healing tool.

Resistance towards art therapy in inner child healing is common and can arise from various factors such as fear of judgment, self-doubt, trauma triggers, and limited experience with art. Overcoming this resistance is essential for individuals to fully engage in the healing process. Strategies for overcoming resistance include acknowledging resistance, practicing mindfulness, starting small, building a support system, reframing negative beliefs, using art as a tool for self-expression, and being gentle with oneself. By using these strategies, individuals can overcome their resistance towards art therapy and begin to unlock the power of creativity in their inner child healing journey. Remember, healing is a journey, and it is important to be patient and kind to oneself along the way.

Chapter 14: Healing Your Inner Child with Spiritual Practices

Inner child healing is a therapeutic process that involves addressing and healing emotional wounds that were formed during childhood. While traditional therapy methods such as talk therapy and art therapy can be effective, there are other methods that can be incorporated to enhance the healing process. Spiritual practices can play a significant role in inner child healing, providing individuals with a deeper sense of connection, purpose, and healing.

In this chapter, we will explore the role of spirituality in inner child healing, including what spirituality is and the benefits of incorporating spiritual practices into the healing process. We will also discuss strategies for using spiritual practices in inner child work and provide examples of spiritual practices for healing inner child wounds.

Additionally, we will discuss the role of faith in inner child healing and how it can be incorporated into the healing journey. We will explore how faith can help with inner child healing and provide tips for incorporating faith into the healing process.

Overall, this chapter aims to provide individuals with a deeper understanding of the role of spirituality and faith in inner child healing. By incorporating spiritual practices and faith into the healing journey, individuals can experience a greater sense of connection to themselves, others, and a higher power, ultimately leading to greater healing and well-being.

Understanding Spirituality in Inner Child Healing

Spiritual practices can play a significant role in inner child healing, providing individuals with a deeper sense of connection, purpose, and healing. In this heading, we will explore the meaning of spirituality, its role in inner child healing, and the benefits of incorporating spirituality into the healing journey.

What is Spirituality?

Spirituality is a broad and personal term that can mean different things to different people. At its core, spirituality is often described as a belief in something beyond oneself, a sense of connection to a higher power, and a quest for meaning and purpose in life. It can involve practices such as meditation, prayer, mindfulness, or other spiritual practices.

Spirituality can also involve a sense of connection to others and the world around us. It can help individuals to feel a greater sense of compassion, empathy, and interconnectedness with all living beings. For many people, spirituality is an important aspect of their daily lives and provides a framework for their beliefs, values, and actions.

Spirituality can be practiced in many ways and can take on many different forms. Some individuals may find spirituality through organized religion, while others may find it through nature or other forms of connection to the world around them. Ultimately, spirituality is a deeply personal experience that can bring individuals a sense of peace, purpose, and connection to something greater than themselves.

Benefits of Spirituality for Inner Child Healing

- Greater Sense of Connection: Spirituality can provide individuals with a greater sense of connection to themselves, others, and a higher power. This sense of connection can help individuals to feel less alone and isolated, which can be especially important for those who have experienced childhood trauma. When individuals feel connected to something greater than themselves, they can feel more supported and less alone in their healing journey.

Spirituality can also help individuals to feel more connected to others, which can provide a sense of community and support.

- Increased Self-Awareness: Spirituality can also lead to increased self-awareness. By exploring their beliefs, values, and purpose in life, individuals can gain a greater understanding of themselves and their inner child wounds. This increased self-awareness can help individuals to identify their triggers and patterns of behavior, allowing them to make positive changes in their lives. Spirituality can also help individuals to gain insight into their past experiences and how they have shaped their current beliefs and behaviors.

- Greater Resilience: Spirituality can provide individuals with a greater sense of resilience, allowing them to cope better with life's challenges. This can be especially important for those who have experienced childhood trauma and may struggle with feelings of vulnerability and fear. Spirituality can provide individuals with a sense of hope and optimism, helping them to see beyond their current struggles and difficulties. By connecting with a higher power or a sense of purpose, individuals can feel more empowered to overcome adversity and move forward in their healing journey.

- Sense of Meaning and Purpose: Spirituality can also provide individuals with a sense of meaning and purpose in life. This can help individuals to find greater fulfillment and satisfaction in their daily lives. By connecting with a higher power or a sense of purpose, individuals can gain a greater understanding of their place in the world and how they can make a positive impact. This sense of meaning and purpose can be especially important for those who may have struggled with feelings of worthlessness or hopelessness as a result of childhood trauma.

- Greater Emotional Regulation: Spirituality can also provide individuals with greater emotional regulation. By practicing mindfulness or other spiritual practices, individuals can learn to regulate their emotions and respond to stressors in a more effective way. This can be especially important for those who have experienced childhood trauma and may struggle with intense emotions. By practicing mindfulness or other spiritual practices, individuals can learn to cultivate a sense of inner peace and calm, allowing them to respond to life's challenges in a more centered and balanced way.

Overall, spirituality can play a significant role in inner child healing. By providing individuals with a greater sense of connection, self-awareness, resilience, meaning, and emotional regulation, spirituality can enhance the healing process and support individuals in their journey toward greater well-being.

Using Spiritual Practices in Inner Child Healing

Inner child healing is a process that involves healing emotional wounds that were formed during childhood. While traditional therapy methods such as talk therapy and art therapy can be effective, there are other methods that can be incorporated to enhance the healing process. Spiritual practices can play a significant role in inner child healing, providing individuals with a deeper sense of connection, purpose, and healing. In this article, we will explore strategies for using spiritual practices in inner child work.

Strategies for Using Spiritual Practices in Inner Child Work

Here are the strategies for using spiritual practices in inner child work.

1. Start Small: When incorporating spiritual practices into inner child work, it can be helpful to start small. It can be overwhelming to try to incorporate too many practices at once, so it is important to choose one or two practices to focus on initially. For example, an individual may start with a daily mindfulness meditation practice or incorporate journaling into their daily routine. By starting small, individuals can build a foundation for their spiritual practice and gradually incorporate additional practices as they become more comfortable.

2. Find What Works for You: It is important to find spiritual practices that resonate with you and align with your personal beliefs and values. There is no one-size-fits-all approach to spiritual practices, so it is important to explore different practices and find what works for you. For example, some individuals may find that prayer is a powerful practice for them, while others may prefer mindfulness meditation or creative expression.

3. Be Consistent: Consistency is key when it comes to incorporating spiritual practices into inner child work. It can be helpful to set aside a specific time each day or week to engage in spiritual practices. This can help to establish a routine and make the practices a regular part of your life. Consistency can also help to deepen your connection to your spiritual practice and enhance the healing process.

4. Incorporate into Daily Routine: Incorporating spiritual practices into your daily routine can be a powerful way to enhance inner child healing. For example, an individual may start each day with a mindfulness meditation practice or end each day with a gratitude practice.

By incorporating spiritual practices into your daily routine, you can create a sense of structure and ritual around your healing journey.

5. Seek Guidance and Support: Seeking guidance and support from others can be helpful when incorporating spiritual practices into inner child work. This can include working with a spiritual mentor, joining a spiritual community, or seeking guidance from a therapist or counselor. It can be helpful to connect with others who share similar beliefs and values, as this can provide a sense of connection and support.

6. Practice Self-Compassion: Inner child work can be a challenging and emotional process, and it is important to practice self-compassion when engaging in spiritual practices. It is important to be gentle and patient with yourself and to acknowledge that healing takes time. It can be helpful to practice self-care and engage in activities that bring you joy and fulfillment.

Incorporating spiritual practices into inner child work can be a powerful way to enhance the healing journey. By starting small, finding what works for you, being consistent, incorporating it into your daily routine, seeking guidance and support, and practicing self-compassion, you can deepen your connection to your spiritual practice and experience a deeper sense of healing and well-being.

Examples of Spiritual Practices for Healing Inner Child Wounds

Here are examples of spiritual practices for healing inner child wounds.

Mindfulness Meditation: Mindfulness meditation is a powerful spiritual practice for healing inner child wounds. By practicing mindfulness meditation, individuals can gain a greater sense of self-awareness, emotional regulation, and a sense of inner peace. This can be especially helpful for those who have experienced childhood trauma and may struggle with intense emotions or feelings of disconnection. To practice mindfulness meditation, individuals can find a quiet space and focus on their breath, observing their thoughts and emotions without judgment.

Prayer: Prayer is a common spiritual practice that can be used to heal inner child wounds. Prayer involves connecting with a higher power or spiritual force and can provide individuals with a sense of hope, guidance, and support. This can be especially helpful for those who have experienced childhood trauma and may struggle with feelings of worthlessness or disconnection. To practice prayer, individuals can find a quiet space and connect with their higher power through words, thoughts, or feelings.

Journaling: Journaling is another spiritual practice that can be beneficial for healing inner child wounds. By journaling, individuals can explore their thoughts and emotions in a safe and non-judgmental space. This can be especially helpful for those who have difficulty expressing themselves verbally or who struggle to connect with their emotions. Journaling can also help individuals to gain insight into their past experiences and how they have shaped their current beliefs and behaviors. To practice journaling, individuals can set aside time each day to write down their thoughts and feelings.

Creative Expression: Creative expression is another spiritual practice that can be used to heal inner child wounds. By engaging in creative activities such as art, music, or dance, individuals can tap into their inner creativity and self-expression. This can be especially helpful for those who have difficulty expressing themselves verbally or who struggle with negative self-talk or self-doubt. To practice creative expression, individuals can find a creative outlet that resonates with them and make time for it regularly.

Nature Walks: Nature walks can also be a powerful spiritual practice for healing inner child wounds. By connecting with nature, individuals can gain a sense of peace, grounding, and connection to something greater than themselves. This can be especially helpful for those who have experienced childhood trauma and may struggle with feelings of disconnection or isolation. To practice nature walks, individuals can make time to spend time in nature regularly, whether it's going for a walk in the park or spending time in the wilderness.

Gratitude Practice: Gratitude is a powerful spiritual practice that can be used to heal inner child wounds. By practicing gratitude, individuals can shift their focus from negative emotions and experiences to the positive aspects of their lives. This can help individuals to gain a greater sense of perspective and appreciation for the good in their lives, which can enhance their overall sense of well-being. To practice gratitude, individuals can set aside time each day to reflect on what they are grateful for and express gratitude to others.

Overall, there are many examples of spiritual practices that can be used to heal inner child wounds. By incorporating spiritual practices such as mindfulness meditation, prayer, journaling, creative expression, nature walks, and gratitude practice, individuals can enhance their healing journey and experience a deeper sense of connection, purpose, and healing.

The Role of Faith in Inner Child Healing

Faith can play a significant role in inner child healing, providing individuals with a deeper sense of connection, purpose, and healing. Many individuals find comfort and guidance in their faith when dealing with emotional wounds from childhood. In this article, we will explore the role of faith in inner child healing and how to incorporate faith into the healing journey.

How Faith Can Help with Inner Child Healing

Sense of Connection

Faith can provide individuals with a sense of connection to something greater than themselves. This connection can be with a higher power, a community of believers, or a shared set of values and beliefs. For individuals who have experienced childhood trauma, this sense of connection can be especially important, as they may struggle with feelings of isolation, disconnection, or mistrust.

Through faith, individuals can find a sense of belonging and community. This can involve connecting with a faith community such as a church, mosque, or temple or simply feeling a connection to a higher power. This sense of connection can provide individuals with a sense of support and validation, which can enhance the healing journey.

For example, an individual who has experienced childhood trauma may feel disconnected from themselves and others. They may struggle with feelings of worthlessness or lack of purpose. By connecting with a faith community or higher power, they may begin to feel a sense of belonging and purpose. They may find that their faith provides them with a sense of meaning and direction, which can enhance their sense of well-being and help them to heal from their emotional wounds.

Overall, the sense of connection provided by faith can be a powerful tool in inner child healing. By providing individuals with a sense of belonging and community, faith can enhance the healing journey and provide individuals with a deeper sense of connection to themselves and others.

Sense of Purpose

Faith can also provide individuals with a sense of purpose in life. For individuals who have experienced childhood trauma, this sense of purpose can be especially important, as they may struggle with feelings of worthlessness, lack of direction, or a sense of disconnection from their own lives.

Through faith, individuals can find a sense of direction and mean in their lives. This can involve connecting with a higher power and feeling a sense of guidance or simply feeling a sense of purpose through their shared set of values and beliefs. This sense of purpose can provide individuals with a sense of direction and motivation, which can enhance the healing journey.

For example, an individual who has experienced childhood trauma may struggle with feelings of hopelessness or lack of direction. They may feel disconnected from their own lives and unsure of their purpose. By connecting with their faith, they may begin to feel a sense of guidance and direction. They may find that their faith provides them with a sense of purpose and motivation to move forward in their healing journey.

Overall, the sense of purpose provided by faith can be a powerful tool in inner child healing. By providing individuals with a sense of direction and meaning, faith can enhance the healing journey and provide individuals with a deeper sense of purpose and motivation to move forward in their lives.

Source of Comfort

Faith can provide individuals with a source of comfort and strength during difficult times. For individuals who have experienced childhood trauma, this source of comfort can be especially important, as they may struggle with intense emotions or feelings of hopelessness.

Through faith, individuals can find a sense of peace and comfort in the midst of difficult emotions or circumstances. This can involve connecting with a higher power and feeling a sense of support and guidance or simply finding comfort in their shared set of values and beliefs. This source of comfort can provide individuals with a sense of hope and resilience, which can enhance the healing journey.

For example, an individual who has experienced childhood trauma may struggle with intense emotions such as anxiety, fear, or depression. By connecting with their faith, they may find a sense of peace and comfort. They may find that their faith provides them with a sense of support and hope, which can help them to cope with difficult emotions and move forward in their healing journey.

Overall, the source of comfort provided by faith can be a powerful tool in inner child healing. By providing individuals with a sense of peace and resilience, faith can enhance the healing journey and provide individuals with a deeper sense of hope and support during difficult times.

Forgiveness

Faith can also provide individuals with a sense of forgiveness and compassion. For individuals who have experienced childhood trauma, forgiveness can be especially challenging, as they may struggle with intense emotions such as anger, resentment, or bitterness.

Through faith, individuals can find a sense of forgiveness and compassion for themselves and others. This can involve connecting with a higher power and seeking forgiveness for past actions or simply practicing forgiveness towards themselves and others as a way of letting go of negative emotions. This sense of forgiveness can provide individuals with a sense of peace and closure, which can enhance the healing journey.

For example, an individual who has experienced childhood trauma may struggle with feelings of anger or resentment towards a parent or caregiver who caused them harm. By connecting with their faith, they may find a sense of forgiveness towards themselves and the other person. They may find that their faith provides them with a sense of compassion and empathy, which can help them to release negative emotions and move towards a sense of healing and peace.

Overall, the sense of forgiveness provided by faith can be a powerful tool in inner child healing. By providing individuals with a sense of compassion and forgiveness, faith can enhance the healing journey and provide individuals with a deeper sense of peace and closure.

Incorporating Faith into The Healing Journey

Prayer

Prayer is one of the most common and powerful ways to incorporate faith into the healing journey. Prayer involves connecting with a higher power or spiritual force through words, thoughts, or feelings. Prayer can be a deeply personal experience and can provide individuals with a sense of hope, guidance, and support.

Through prayer, individuals can express their feelings, seek guidance, and ask for help in their healing journey. Prayer can provide a sense of peace and comfort, as well as a sense of connection to something greater than oneself. This connection can be especially important for individuals who have experienced childhood trauma and may struggle with feelings of disconnection or isolation.

For example, an individual who has experienced childhood trauma may struggle with feelings of hopelessness or lack of direction. By incorporating prayer into their healing journey, they may find a sense of guidance and support. They may find that prayer provides them with a sense of comfort and peace, which can help them to cope with difficult emotions and move forward in their healing journey.

Overall, prayer can be a powerful tool in inner child healing. By providing individuals with a sense of connection, guidance, and support, prayer can enhance the healing journey and provide individuals with a deeper sense of peace and well-being.

Meditation

Meditation is another way to incorporate faith into the healing journey. Meditation involves focusing one's attention on the present moment without judgment or distraction. By practicing meditation, individuals can gain a greater sense of self-awareness and connect with their inner selves.

Through meditation, individuals can find a sense of peace and calmness, which can be especially helpful for those who have experienced childhood trauma and may struggle with intense emotions or feelings of disconnection. Meditation can help individuals to regulate their emotions and thoughts and to develop a greater sense of self-control.

For example, an individual who has experienced childhood trauma may struggle with intrusive thoughts or emotions. By incorporating meditation into their healing journey, they may find a sense of calmness and control over their thoughts and emotions. They may find that meditation provides them with a sense of inner peace, which can help them to cope with difficult emotions and move forward in their healing journey.

Overall, meditation can be a powerful tool in inner child healing. By providing individuals with a sense of self-awareness and inner peace, meditation can enhance the healing journey and provide individuals with a deeper sense of self-control and emotional regulation.

Scripture Reading

Scripture reading is another way to incorporate faith into the healing journey. Scripture refers to sacred texts or writings that are considered to be authoritative or inspired by a higher power. Scripture reading can provide individuals with guidance and inspiration, as well as a sense of connection to something greater than themselves.

Through scripture reading, individuals can find a sense of meaning and purpose in their lives, as well as a sense of direction and guidance. Scripture can provide individuals with stories of hope and resilience, as well as teachings on forgiveness, compassion, and love.

For example, an individual who has experienced childhood trauma may struggle with feelings of hopelessness or lack of direction. By incorporating scripture reading into their healing journey, they may find a sense of guidance and inspiration. They may find that scripture provides them with a sense of hope and purpose, which can help them to move forward in their healing journey.

Overall, scripture reading can be a powerful tool in inner child healing. By providing individuals with guidance and inspiration, scripture reading can enhance the healing journey and provide individuals with a deeper sense of meaning and purpose in their lives.

Joining a Faith Community

Joining a faith community is another way to incorporate faith into the healing journey. A faith community refers to a group of individuals who share a common set of beliefs and values related to spirituality or religion. Joining a faith community can provide individuals with a sense of belonging, support, and guidance.

Through a faith community, individuals can connect with others who share similar experiences, as well as receive support and guidance from religious leaders or mentors. A faith community can provide a sense of accountability and encouragement, as well as opportunities for service and connection.

For example, an individual who has experienced childhood trauma may struggle with feelings of isolation or disconnection. By joining a faith community, they may find a sense of belonging and support. They may find that the community provides them with a sense of purpose and meaning, as well as opportunities for service and connection.

Overall, joining a faith community can be a powerful tool in inner child healing. By providing individuals with a sense of belonging and support, faith communities can enhance the healing journey and provide individuals with a deeper sense of connection and purpose.

Chapter 15: Healing Your Inner Child with Dreamwork

Welcome to chapter 15 of our series on inner child healing. In this chapter, we will explore the power of dreamwork as a tool for healing your inner child. Dreams have been used for centuries as a means of exploring the unconscious mind and gaining insight into our deepest fears, desires, and emotions.

Dreamwork involves using dreams as a tool for self-exploration and healing. By exploring the symbols, themes, and emotions that arise in our dreams, we can gain a deeper understanding of our inner world and the wounds that may be holding us back.

In this chapter, we will explore the benefits of dreamwork for inner child healing and provide strategies and exercises for incorporating dreamwork into your healing journey. We will also explore the role of dreams in inner child healing and how to incorporate dreamwork into your daily life.

We will begin by defining dreamwork and exploring its benefits for inner child healing. By understanding the power of dreamwork, we can gain a deeper appreciation for its potential as a tool for healing.

Next, we will discuss strategies for using dreamwork in inner child work, including journaling, visualization, and active imagination. These techniques can help you to explore the symbols, themes, and emotions that arise in your dreams and gain a deeper understanding of your inner world.

We will also provide examples of dreamwork exercises for healing inner child wounds, such as reimagining past experiences and exploring archetypal symbols. By incorporating these exercises into your dreamwork practice, you can gain greater insight into your inner world and move towards healing.

Finally, we will explore the role of dreams in inner child healing and how to incorporate dreamwork into your daily life. By paying attention to your dreams and using them as a tool for self-exploration, you can gain a deeper understanding of your inner world and move towards healing your inner child.

Understanding Dreamwork

What is Dreamwork?

Dreamwork is a process of exploring dreams as a tool for self-exploration and healing. Dreams are a natural part of the human experience, and they can provide a window into the unconscious mind. Dreamwork involves paying attention to the symbols, themes, and emotions that arise in our dreams and using them to gain a deeper understanding of our inner world.

Dreamwork can take many forms, including journaling, visualization, and active imagination. These techniques can help individuals to explore the symbols, themes, and emotions that arise in their dreams and gain a deeper understanding of their inner world.

Journaling is a common technique used in dream work. By writing down dreams as soon as they wake up, individuals can capture the symbols, themes, and emotions that arise in their dreams. This can help individuals to explore the meaning behind their dreams and gain insight into their inner world.

Visualization is another technique used in dream work. By revisiting dreams through visualization, individuals can explore the symbols, themes, and emotions that arise in their dreams and gain a deeper understanding of their inner world.

An active imagination is a technique used in dreamwork that involves exploring dreams through creative expression. This can involve drawing or painting the symbols and themes that arise in dreams or even acting out dreams through movement or drama. By engaging with dreams in a creative and imaginative way, individuals can gain a deeper understanding of their inner world and move towards healing.

Benefits of Dreamwork for Inner Child Healing

Dreamwork can provide numerous benefits for inner child healing. By exploring the symbols, themes, and emotions that arise in our dreams, we can gain a deeper understanding of our inner world and move toward healing. Here are some of the key benefits of dreamwork for inner child healing:

- Insight: Dreams can provide a window into the unconscious mind, allowing us to gain insight into our deepest fears, desires, and emotions. By exploring the symbols, themes, and emotions that arise in our dreams, we can gain a deeper understanding of our inner world and the wounds that may be holding us back.

- Self-awareness: Dreamwork can help individuals to become more self-aware and in tune with their emotions and inner experiences. By paying attention to their dreams and exploring the symbols and themes that arise, individuals can gain a greater understanding of their inner world and their relationship to the outside world.

- Emotional regulation: Dreams can be a powerful tool for emotional regulation. By exploring the emotions that arise in our dreams, we can learn to regulate our emotions and gain a greater sense of emotional stability and well-being.

- Healing: Dreamwork can be a powerful tool for healing childhood wounds and traumas. By exploring the symbols, themes, and emotions that arise in our dreams, we can gain a deeper understanding of the wounds that may be holding us back and move toward healing.

- Creativity: Dreamwork can be a highly creative process involving visualization, journaling, and other forms of creative expression. By engaging with dreams in a creative way, individuals can tap into their creativity and move towards greater self-expression and self-discovery.

- Spiritual growth: Dreams can also provide a powerful tool for spiritual growth and development. By exploring the symbols and themes that arise in our dreams, we can gain a deeper understanding of our spiritual path and our relationship with the divine.

Overall, dreamwork can provide numerous benefits for inner child healing. By exploring the symbols, themes, and emotions that arise in our dreams, we can gain a deeper understanding of our inner world and move toward healing and well-being. Dreamwork can provide individuals with a greater sense of self-awareness, emotional regulation, creativity, and spiritual growth.

Using Dreamwork in Inner Child Healing

Dreamwork can be a powerful tool in inner child healing. By exploring the symbols, themes, and emotions that arise in our dreams, we can gain a deeper understanding of our inner world and move toward healing.

Strategies For Using Dreamwork in Inner Child Work

Here are some strategies for using dreamwork in inner child work:

- Keep a dream journal: Keeping a dream journal is one of the most common and effective ways to use dreamwork in inner child work. By writing down dreams as soon as you wake up, you can capture the symbols, themes, and emotions that arise in your dreams. This can help you to explore the meaning behind your dreams and gain insight into your inner world.

- Reflect on your dreams: After writing down your dreams, take some time to reflect on them. Consider the symbols, themes, and emotions that arose in your dreams. Ask yourself what these symbols and themes might represent and how they relate to your inner child.

- Use visualization: Visualization is a powerful technique for exploring dreams. After reflecting on your dreams, try to visualize the symbols and themes that arose in your dreams. Imagine yourself in the dream and explore the feelings and emotions that arise. This can help you to gain a deeper understanding of the meaning behind your dreams and move towards healing.

- Explore archetypes: Archetypes are universal symbols that represent common themes and experiences. By exploring archetypes in your dreams, you can gain insight into your inner world and the wounds that may be holding you back. For example, the archetype of the wounded child may represent your inner child and the wounds they have experienced.

- Engage in active imagination: Active imagination involves exploring dreams through creative expression. This can involve drawing or painting the symbols and themes that arise in your dreams or even acting out dreams through movement or drama. By engaging with dreams in a creative and imaginative way, you can gain a deeper understanding of your inner world and move towards healing.

- Work with a therapist: Working with a therapist who is trained in dreamwork can be an effective way to use dreamwork in inner child healing. A therapist can help you to explore the symbols, themes, and emotions that arise in your dreams and provide guidance and support as you move toward healing.

Overall, dreamwork can be a powerful tool in inner child healing. By using strategies such as keeping a dream journal, reflecting on your dreams, using visualization, exploring archetypes, engaging in active imagination, and working with a therapist, you can gain a deeper understanding of your inner world and move towards healing and well-being.

Dreamwork Exercises for Healing Inner Child Wounds

Dreamwork can be a powerful tool for healing inner child wounds. Here are some dreamwork exercises for healing inner child wounds and an example for each exercise:

1. Reimagining past experiences: This exercise involves revisiting past experiences from childhood and imagining how they could have played out differently. By reimagining past experiences in a positive way, you can gain a greater sense of empowerment and healing. For example, if you had a traumatic experience with a caregiver as a child, you might reimagine the experience as one where the caregiver was supportive and loving. You might visualize yourself feeling safe and cared for at that moment.

2. Identifying and working with recurring dreams: Recurring dreams are often a sign that there is an unresolved issue or wound that needs to be addressed. By identifying and working with recurring dreams, you can gain insight into the wounds that may be holding you back and move toward healing. For example, if you have recurring dreams about being abandoned or rejected, you might explore the feelings and emotions that arise in the dream and consider how they relate to your inner child.

3. Exploring archetypal symbols: Archetypal symbols, such as the mother, father, or wounded child, can provide insight into our deepest fears, desires, and emotions. By exploring archetypal symbols in your dreams, you can gain a deeper understanding of your inner world and the wounds that may be holding you back. For example, if you dream about a mother figure who is nurturing and caring, you might explore the emotions that arise in the dream and consider how they relate to your relationship with your own mother.

4. Creating a dream collage: A dream collage involves collecting images that represent the symbols, themes, and emotions that arise in your dreams and creating a visual representation of them. This can help you to explore your dreams in a creative and imaginative way and gain a deeper understanding of your inner world. For example, you might collect images of a wounded child, a caring mother, and a safe and secure home and arrange them in a collage that represents your inner child and their needs.

5. Engaging in active imagination: Active imagination involves exploring dreams through creative expression. This can involve drawing or painting the symbols and themes that arise in your dreams or even acting out dreams through movement or drama. By engaging with dreams in a creative and imaginative way, you can gain a deeper understanding of your inner world and move towards healing. For example, if you dream about a traumatic experience with a caregiver, you might act out the experience through role-play or create a painting that represents the emotions and feelings that arise in the dream.

The Role of Dreams in Inner Child Healing

By exploring the symbols, themes, and emotions that arise in our dreams, we can gain insight into our inner world and the wounds that may be holding us back. Dreams can provide a safe space for exploring difficult emotions and experiences, and they can offer valuable insights into our deepest fears, desires, and emotions.

One way in which dreams can help with inner child healing is by providing insight into the inner child. Dreams can reveal the wounds and traumas that the inner child has experienced, and by exploring these symbols, themes, and emotions, we can gain a deeper understanding of our inner child and their needs. For example, a dream about a lost and scared child may represent our own inner child and their need for safety and security.

Another way in which dreams can help with inner child healing is by offering a safe space for exploration. Dreams offer a contained environment in which we can experience intense emotions and process difficult experiences. This can help us to work through emotions and experiences that may feel overwhelming in waking life. By exploring these emotions and experiences in our dreams, we can gain insight into our inner world and move toward healing.

Dreams can also illuminate patterns and themes that may be present in our inner world. Recurring dreams and themes can provide insight into the wounds and traumas that we may be carrying with us. By exploring these patterns and themes, we can gain a deeper understanding of our inner world and the wounds that may be holding us back. For example, recurring dreams about being abandoned or rejected may indicate a deep-seated fear of rejection or abandonment.

Conclusion

In conclusion, "Healing Your Inner Child: Cognitive Behavioral Therapy Strategies to Address Trauma and Abandonment Wounds | How to Unlock Emotional Freedom and Self-Love" offers a comprehensive guide to healing from childhood wounds and building a strong foundation of self-love and emotional freedom.

Throughout this book, we have explored the concept of inner child healing, which involves addressing and healing the wounds and traumas that individuals may have experienced during their childhood. We have discussed the impact of childhood wounds on adult life, including their effects on self-esteem, relationships, and emotional regulation.

We have also examined various cognitive-behavioral therapy (CBT) strategies and techniques, such as identifying negative thought patterns, replacing negative thoughts with positive ones, and addressing negative self-talk. Other tools and techniques for inner child healing, such as mindfulness, visualization, journaling, and self-compassion exercises, were also discussed.

Furthermore, we have explored specific types of childhood wounds, including abandonment, neglect, and abuse, and provided strategies for addressing each of these wounds through inner child work. The role of positive affirmations, self-love, and spirituality in inner child healing was also examined, as well as the use of art therapy and dreamwork in healing inner child wounds.

Embarking on an inner child healing journey can be challenging and emotionally difficult. It requires a willingness to confront painful memories and emotions, to be vulnerable and open, and to persevere through resistance and setbacks. However, the rewards of this work are profound - increased self-awareness, self-love, and overall well-being.

It is important to remember that healing is a journey, and progress may not always be linear. There may be times when it feels difficult or overwhelming, but it is essential to be patient and compassionate with yourself throughout the process. Remember that every step you take towards healing your inner child is a step towards a healthier and more fulfilling life.

We encourage readers to continue to explore and utilize the strategies and techniques presented in this book, as well as seek additional support and resources as needed. By prioritizing your inner child healing, you are investing in your own well-being and creating a more positive and fulfilling life.

We also recommend exploring additional resources for continued growth and healing. There are many excellent books, websites, and therapy resources available to support you on your journey.

Here are some recommendations for continued growth and healing:

Books:

- "Healing the Child Within" by Charles Whitfield
- "The Courage to Heal" by Ellen Bass and Laura Davis
- "The Body Keeps the Score" by Bessel van der Kolk
- "Running on Empty" by Jonice Webb
- "Parenting from the Inside Out" by Daniel J. Siegel and Mary Hartzell

Websites:

- The National Child Traumatic Stress Network: https://www.nctsn.org/
- The International Society for the Study of Trauma and Dissociation: https://www.isst-d.org/
- The Sidran Institute: https://www.sidran.org/

Therapy resources:

- Cognitive Behavioral Therapy (CBT)
- Eye Movement Desensitization and Reprocessing (EMDR)
- Trauma-Focused Cognitive Behavioral Therapy (TF-CBT)
- Dialectical Behavioral Therapy (DBT)
- Art Therapy

By continuing to prioritize your emotional well-being and investing in your inner child healing, you can unlock a greater sense of emotional freedom and self-love in your life.

Printed in Great Britain
by Amazon

25888961R00084